A
GOURMET'S
GUIDE TO

CHOCOLATE

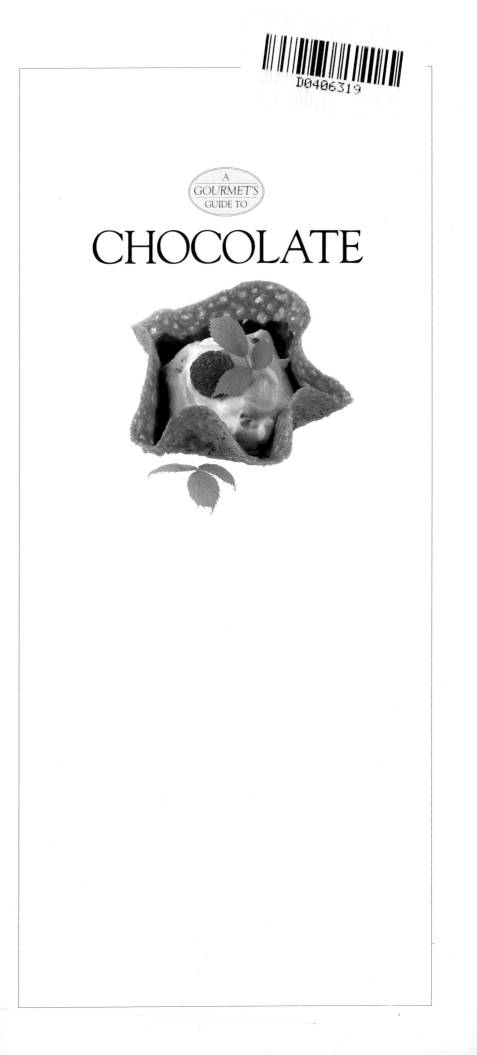

A
GOURMET'S
GUIDE TO

CHOCOLATE

LESLEY MACKLEY
&
CAROLE HANDSLIP

Photography by
SUE ATKINSON

HPBooks
a division of
PRICE STERN SLOAN
Los Angeles

ANOTHER BEST SELLING VOLUME FROM HPBOOKS

HPBooks
A division of Price Stern Sloan, Inc.
360 North La Cienega Boulevard
Los Angeles, California 90048

9 8 7 6 5 4 3 2 1

This book was created by Merehurst Limited
Ferry House, 51/57 Lacy Road, London SW15 1PR

© Salamander Books Ltd., 1989

Commissioned and Directed by Merehurst Limited
Photographer: Sue Atkinson
Food Stylists: Maria Kelly & Carolyn Russel
Home Economist: Carole Handslip
Color reproduction by Contemporary Lithoplates Ltd.
Printed in Belgium by Proost International Book Production, Turnhout

Library of Congress Cataloging-in-Publication Data

Mackley, Lesley.
    A gourmet's guide to chocolate / by Lesley Mackley & Carole
Handslip.

    p.   cm.
    ISBN 0-89586-853-9
    1. Cookery (Chocolate)   I. Handslip, Carole.   II. Title.
TX767.C5M33   1990
641.6'374—dc20   89-19743
                                                            CIP

Contents

Introduction

Chocolate has been valued and enjoyed all over the world for centuries, but the chocolate we know today bears little resemblance to that consumed in such great quantities by the Emperor Montezuma in the 16th century. There are few people who can resist a chocolate cake or dessert, and for some it is almost an addiction. This is hardly surprising, for chocolate contains a natural amphetamine which stimulates the central nervous system to produce a feeling of well-being.

Choosing the right chocolate for a particular recipe can be confusing. In this book, you'll find descriptions of the different types of chocolate available, with instructions for melting and molding chocolate successfully, plus ideas for making all kinds of chocolate decorations.

A collection of recipes—guaranteed to delight all chocolate lovers—completes the book. There are variations of traditional favorites, as well as many new and interesting ideas for mouthwatering desserts, tempting cakes and pastries, sweets and beverages. From elaborate concoctions to some very simple ideas, there are recipes for every occasion. Many can be prepared in advance and quite a few require no cooking at all.

The History of Chocolate

The cacao or cocoa tree is native to South America where it has been cultivated since the 7th century by many people, including the Aztecs, Mayans and Incas. They brewed a drink from cocoa beans, and valued the beans so highly they were also used as currency.

The first Europeans to see the cocoa bean were those on Columbus's fourth voyage in 1502. He returned to Spain with a collection of treasures from the New World, among which were some dark-brown beans, but no one knew what to do with them. It wasn't until twenty years later, when the Spanish conquistador Hernando Cortez arrived in Mexico, that the pleasures to be derived from the cocoa bean were discovered.

Cortez found the Emperor of the Aztecs, Montezuma, consuming up to fifty cups a day of a bitter, pungent drink, called *cacahuatl* or *xocoatl*, from a golden goblet. The drink was believed to be an aphrodisiac, and the beans from which it was brewed a gift from the gods. The enterprising Cortez took some cocoa beans with him when he returned to Spain (this time taking the method of preparing them too). On the trip home, he planted some of the beans in Africa.

The Spanish king and his court were enchanted by this new dark, rich drink and, having sweetened it with sugar and flavored it with vanilla and cinnamon, they jealously guarded the secrets of its delights for over a hundred years.

In 1606, the secret leaked out when Antonio Carletti took the recipe to Italy. From that point on, the pleasures of drinking chocolate spread quickly across Europe.

At the beginning of the 17th century, the exotic new chocolate drink was an expensive luxury greatly appreciated only by the aristocrats at many European courts, but soon chocolate houses were springing up all over Europe as meeting places for the fashionable and learned. White's and The Cocoa Tree were the most popular chocolate houses in London, frequented by Samuel Pepys and many poets, playwrights and would-be politicians.

The chocolate drink that enjoyed such popularity then was made from a crumbly coarse paste that had a high fat content. Two centuries later, in 1828, a Dutchman named Van Houten invented a press to extract the fat or cocoa butter from the beans, leaving behind a powder that could be dissolved in water to make a chocolate drink. Later, in 1847, the English firm, Fry & Sons, added sugar and chocolate liquor to the cocoa butter to produce the first eating chocolate.

In the early days all eating chocolate was plain, with a rough, grainy texture. The first milk chocolate was made in Switzerland in 1876, and the Swiss continued to improve their recipe until it became the smooth melting chocolate we know today.

Since then, our appetite for chocolate has continued to increase, with chocolate for eating having long ago overtaken chocolate for drinking in popularity.

Producing Chocolate

The cacao tree *(Theobroma cacao)* is only cultivated in the tropical zone within 20° of the equator. West Africa produces 60% of the world's supply of cocoa, while Brazil is the largest producer in South America. The trees start producing pods when they are three to five years old. They bloom throughout the year but only twenty to thirty of the 10,000 blossoms produced by each tree develop into fully grown, spindle-shaped fruits or pods. These form on the trunk and thickest branches of the tree. Each one contains thirty to forty white or purple seeds—the cocoa beans.

After harvesting, the pods are slit open and the beans and pulp scooped out and piled into heaps on banana or plaintain leaves. They are covered with a layer of leaves and left to ferment for five to six days. As the temperature in the heap rises, the pulp

The basis of chocolate: cocoa beans, milk and sugar.

becomes liquid and drains away. During this process the beans turn dark brown, the shells become thinner and the cocoa flavor really develops.

After fermentation, the beans are left to dry in the sun, then shipped to manufacturers for processing.

The first processing stage is roasting, which further develops the cocoa flavor. After roasting, the kernels or nibs are extracted from the beans and ground. The friction of grinding extracts the cocoa butter, leaving a thick paste called chocolate liquor. When cooled, this hardens to form unsweetened cooking chocolate. Further pressing of the nibs extracts even more cocoa butter, and the remaining solid cake is ground to form cocoa powder.

To make semisweet eating chocolate, extra cocoa butter and sugar are added to the chocolate liquor. To make milk chocolate, milk, in a dried form, is also added.

The next stage is called conching. The semiliquid mixture is poured into machines which grind, mix and slightly heat the ingredients for several days. This evaporates moisture, improves the texture and develops the flavor.

Before chocolate is molded in bars or used for coating purposes, it is tempered by cooling very carefully to 79F (26C). This further improves the texture, gloss and keeping qualities of chocolate.

Types of Chocolate

Baking chocolate is unsweetened chocolate for cooking. It is excellent used in baked goods.

Semisweet chocolate is the most useful type for cooking, as it gives a good strong chocolate flavor. However, quality varies considerably according to the proportion of cocoa solids listed in the ingredients. The higher the percentage of cocoa solids, the better the chocolate. It should contain a minimum of 34%—the best chocolate contains 50% or more—so check this on the package. Price is a good indication of quality; it is worth buying the best you can afford, for it will show in the texture, flavor and appearance of the finished dish.

Milk chocolate is not satisfactory for use in cooking, but melted it may be piped onto semisweet chocolate for a decorative effect. It may also be used for molding Easter eggs for children, who often prefer the flavor of milk chocolate.

White chocolate is not really chocolate at all, as it comprises cocoa butter, milk and sugar, but contains no chocolate liquor. It is not usually used for cooking because of its lack of flavor, but its creamy texture makes it suitable for use in cold desserts such as mousses. It gives an interesting contrast when combined with semisweet chocolate.

Couverture is generally only available to professional confectioners. It has a high cocoa butter content and flows very smoothly, making it ideal for coating purposes. It must be tempered, page 9, before use.

Compound or confectionery coatings contain vegetable oil instead of added cocoa butter, which makes it considerably cheaper than true chocolate. For most purposes the flavor and texture are inferior, and not recommended for use in this collection of recipes.

However, for the less experienced cook, compound or confectionery coatings are easier to work with. They are more difficult to spoil when melting, they are more fluid and therefore easier to use for coating. They set very quickly.

Adding one tablespoon oil to every eight ounces melted semisweet chocolate makes it equally fluid for coating and dipping.

Unsweetened cocoa powder is a convenient and inexpensive way of achieving a strong chocolate flavor in baking, but it is not suitable for use in uncooked dishes. A good substitute for bitter chocolate is a mixture of three tablespoons unsweetened cocoa powder and one tablespoon butter. Add one tablespoon sugar to provide a substitute for semisweet chocolate.

Sweetened chocolate powder is a mixture of unsweetened cocoa powder and sugar. It is too sweet for use in cooking unless the sugar in the recipe is reduced accordingly.

Storing Chocolate

Semisweet and milk chocolate have a shelf life of about one year, but white chocolate tends to deteriorate after about eight months. The shelf life is, of course, dependent upon the chocolate being stored in the correct conditions. It should be well wrapped and stored in a cool place, but not the refrigerator. Chocolate stored at below 55F (13C) will usually develop a bloom, and sweat when transferred to room temperature. When chocolate is stored above 70F (21C), it will also develop a bloom.

Bloom is a greyish-white coating which appears on the surface of chocolate. It affects the appearance but does not impair the flavor, nor is it an indication that the chocolate has deteriorated. Fat bloom is caused by heating and cooling chocolate; it is greasy and easily rubbed off. Sugar bloom shows a white crust of sugar crystals on chocolate which has been stored in a refrigerator; it cannot be removed.

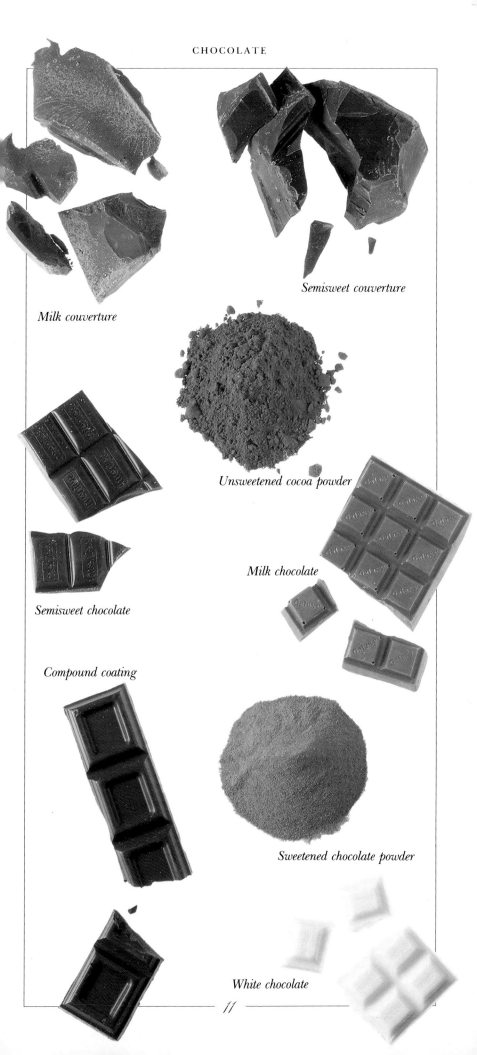

Milk couverture

Semisweet couverture

Unsweetened cocoa powder

Semisweet chocolate

Milk chocolate

Compound coating

Sweetened chocolate powder

White chocolate

The Alternate Chocolate — Carob

Although processed carob and chocolate look similar, they are not related in any way. Carob is not chocolate at all—it is a member of the legume family.

Carob is grown all over the Mediterranean and in the United States. It can take up to fifty years for a carob tree to reach its full height, and up to fifteen years before it produces fruit regularly. The flowers develop into pods which initially resemble fava beans and eventually develop into dark-brown leathery pods with a glossy surface. They are harvested between September and November.

After cleaning the pods, the seeds are separated from the pulp and processed to make a natural gum which is used as a gelling agent, stabilizer or emulsifier in many food products, pharmaceuticals and cosmetics. The pod is then roasted, milled and sieved to produce carob powder, in which form it is ready for use in cooking.

Powdered carob is made into bars by mixing with sugar, vegetable fats, skimmed milk powder, lecithin and flavoring.

Carob has been popular with health food enthusiasts for some years, as it is rich in vitamins and minerals, contains no refined sugar, theobromine, caffeine or oxalic acid and contains fewer calories than chocolate. It is available as a powder or in bars, some of which have added flavoring or nuts.

Carob can be substituted for chocolate in many recipes, although when melted it will not have the shiny finish of chocolate. When used in cooking, it has a mild chocolate flavor and pale color. However, for the chocolate lover and connoisseur, there is no substitute for the real thing.

How to Melt Chocolate

Great care must be taken when melting chocolate, as it scorches very easily if overheated and will develop into hard, grainy lumps. This will also happen if any liquid or steam comes into contact with the chocolate while it is melting.

Chocolate can be safely melted with a small amount of liquid if they are put into the bowl together. It will melt more evenly and quickly if it is broken, chopped or cut in small, even pieces. Do not stir the chocolate until it has melted, and even then stir it very gently. If by mischance the chocolate does develop hard, grainy lumps, it can sometimes be restored by adding a little vegetable oil.

Chocolate can also be added to a large quantity of hot liquid and left to melt, without stirring. Stir when completely melted to make a very smooth mixture.

White chocolate is particularly sensitive to heat; therefore, extra care is needed when melting. When using the microwave method, next column, set the oven on 50% power and cook in one to two minute bursts, stirring the chocolate at each interval.

The following are the most successful ways of melting chocolate.

Over hot water: Place chocolate in a bowl set over a saucepan of simmering water; the bottom of the bowl must not touch the water. Remove pan from heat and let stand until chocolate has melted.

In an oven: Place chocolate in a shallow dish in a 225F (110C) oven. Leave until chocolate is soft.

In a plastic bag: This is a convenient way of melting a small quantity of chocolate, particularly if it is required for piped decoration. Place chocolate in a heavy-gauge plastic bag, seal and set the bag in hot, not boiling water. When chocolate has melted, cut a corner of the bag and use chocolate as required.

In a microwave: This is a very successful way of melting chocolate. Place chocolate in a microwave-proof bowl and heat about two minutes on full power, stirring occasionally. The exact time depends on the quantity of

Melting chocolate for cake icing and contrast piping.

chocolate, size of bowl and wattage of oven.

Using melted chocolate

Allow melted chocolate to cool slightly. Stir and then combine with other ingredients.

Small quantities of butter or oil may be added to make the chocolate smoother and more fluid, if desired, for icing and dipping.

Add chocolate to other liquid ingredients, rather than pouring other liquids into the chocolate.

When using melted chocolate in cake mixtures, add it after creaming the fat and sugar and before adding the eggs and flour.

For soufflé and mousse mixtures, combine the melted chocolate with the egg yolks and flavoring before adding the cream and egg whites.

Bought Decorations

Chocolate shell filled with strawberries and whipped cream; chocolate cup filled with coffee mousse mixture.

A vast array of ready-made chocolate decorations are available for effortless finishes.

Chocolate pieces of semisweet or milk chocolate can be added whole to cake or cookies—they retain their shape even when cooked—or used as cake decorations. Chocolate chips can also be melted and used like chocolate in cooking; they are convenient to use as they melt easily.

Chocolate buttons, either plain or covered, are used for decorating children's cakes. They lend themselves to many ideas, such as tiles on a gingerbread roof.

Chocolate flake used whole is an attractive decoration for cakes, drinks and ice creams. Crumbled, it makes a convenient alternative to grated chocolate. Mini flakes are also available in markets.

Chocolate vermicelli (sprinkles) are available in milk and semisweet chocolate. They are extremely convenient for coating the top and sides of cakes, and for sprinkling over ice cream. They are also used for coating chocolate truffles. The kind most usually found in shops is really chocolate coated sugar strands—real chocolate vermicelli is hard to find.

Chocolate cups and shells are available in a variety of shapes and sizes. Larger ones may be filled with cream and fruit, mousse mixtures, or ice cream, while small cups are suitable for filling with liqueur-flavored truffle mixture to serve with coffee at the end of a meal.

Other chocolate decorations can be found in supermarkets in a wide variety of shapes. In addition to those sold specifically for the purpose, there are many chocolates to be found on the confectionery counter which are ideal for giving a decorative finishing touch to cakes, desserts and ice creams. Thin after dinner mints look attractive arranged around the sides of cakes, or they may be cut in triangles to decorate a chocolate mousse.

Stick-shaped chocolates are available in a range of flavors, such as coffee, mint and orange. As well as making excellent decorations for ice cream, they are delicious broken up and incorporated into the ice cream mixture. Thin chocolate wafers may be used as they are or cut in triangles; they also look decorative lightly crumbled over the top of a cake. Animal-shaped chocolates are ideal for decorating children's birthday cakes.

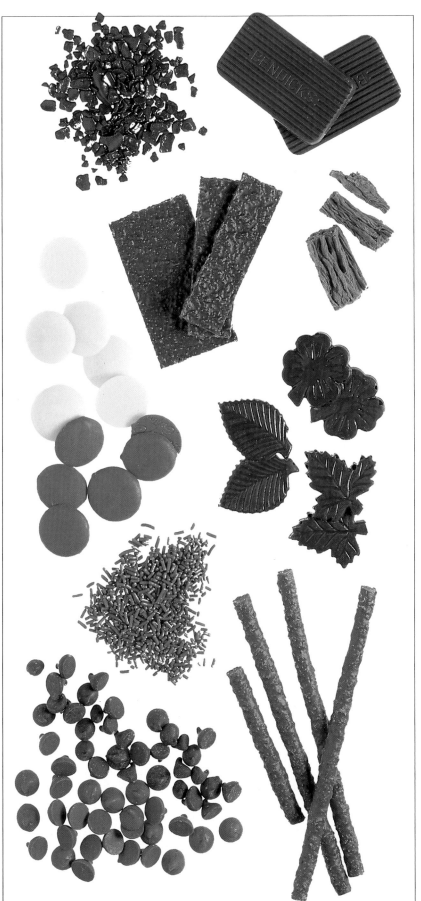

Ready-made chocolate decorations: chocolate pieces, after-dinner mints, flake, buttons, chocolate leaves, sprinkles, chocolate dots and chocolate sticks.

Making Chocolate Decorations

Preparing chocolate leaves.

Homemade chocolate decorations give a professional finish to a variety of cakes, puddings and desserts.

With a little practice, it is possible to produce an endless range of decorations, from the simple to the elaborate. Until you become more experienced and confident, experiment with compound coating as it is easier to work with and any disasters can be remelted and used again. Leave decorations in a cool place to set, but do not put them in a refrigerator or they will develop an unattractive bloom, page 10.

Grated chocolate. One of the most effective chocolate decorations, this is also the simplest. Different effects are achieved according to how coarsely the chocolate is grated.

Use grated chocolate to cover the top and/or sides of a cake which has been iced with whipped cream or butter cream. Roll truffles in finely grated chocolate to coat them.

Grated chocolate can also be sprinkled over a wide variety of desserts and ice cream for a simple finish. For an attractive gâteau or cheesecake topping, sprinkle alternate bands of grated chocolate and sifted powdered sugar over the top, using strips of waxed paper as a guide.

Curls. Use a thick bar of chocolate and make sure it is neither too cold nor too warm. Scrape a vegetable peeler along one long edge of the chocolate bar and allow the curls to fall onto a plate. Lift them carefully onto the dessert to be decorated.

Caraque. Pour a thin layer of melted chocolate over a firm, flat surface, spreading quickly with a knife to smooth. Let stand until set, then, holding the blade of a knife at a 45° angle, push it along the surface of the chocolate to form long scrolls. As the curls form, lift them carefully with the point of a knife. Caraque may be kept in a box in the refrigerator for a short while until required, if necessary.

Leaves. Any fresh leaves may be used—as long as they are not poisonous—but rose leaves are particularly suitable because they have prominent veins and are an attractive shape.

Wash and dry the leaves thoroughly, then brush the underside with melted chocolate, or carefully dip into the chocolate. Place on waxed paper until completely set, then gently lift the tip of the leaf and peel it away from the chocolate.

Chocolate curls, grated chocolate and caraque for decorating cakes.

Piping chocolate: white chocolate drizzled over dark chocolate for an attractive contrast; chocolate feather design applied on coffee glacé icing.

Piped chocolate. Melted chocolate piped directly onto a cake or dessert is a very simple way of achieving a professional finish. It may be piped as writing or a definite pattern, but even easier, and just as effective, is to drizzle a random pattern. Light chocolate piped over dark chocolate, or the two combined in a piped design, look particularly attractive.

To apply a feather design, cover the top of a large cake or individual ones with plain or coffee glacé icing. Immediately pipe on a continuous spiral of melted chocolate, keeping the rings evenly spaced. Draw the point of a knife from the edge of the cake to the center, dividing the cake in quarters, then draw the knife from the center to the edge between these lines to create a feathered effect.

For piping chocolate, use a paper pastry bag with the end snipped off, or a pastry bag fitted with a fine writing nozzle. Or, melt the chocolate in a plastic bag and pipe it from the bag, page 12. Keep your hand as cool as possible while piping, otherwise the chocolate will become too runny. If the chocolate starts to set in the nozzle, return it to a bowl set over hot water and it will soon soften.

Piped decorations. Draw the outline of the required shape on waxed paper as many times as needed. Melt the chocolate and pour into a paper pastry bag. Let stand for a few seconds to cool and thicken slightly, then snip the end of the bag and pipe onto each drawn design. Carefully peel away chocolate from the paper when the chocolate is hard.

Attractive shapes can be made by drawing an outline in dark chocolate, then filling in with milk chocolate when the outline has set. Allow to set hard before removing each shape from the paper.

To make trellis cups, turn a muffin pan upside down and cover the pan with plastic wrap, pressing it down between the cups. Pipe a circle around the top and bottom edges of the cups, then pipe a trellis pattern all over each cup, making sure that all the lines connect. When set, carefully lift the trellis cups off the pan and peel away the plastic wrap.

Selection of piped chocolates outlines, from simple petals and hearts to butterflies and tortoise.

*Preparing chocolate
scallop shells.*

Shapes. Spread a thin layer of melted chocolate onto a sheet of waxed paper. When just set, but not hard, cut out shapes with a cutter or knife.

To cut squares, diamonds, rectangles and triangles use a sharp knife dipped into hot water and dried thoroughly. Cut out shapes by pressing straight down without using a sawing motion. For more complex shapes use a metal cookie cutter, dipped into hot water and dried thoroughly. Aspic cutters are ideal for tiny delicate decorations.

To make chocolate box cakes, cut out squares of thin sponge cake. Spread sides with plain or liqueur-flavored cream and press chocolate squares onto the sides to form a box. The box may be filled with more cream and topped with fruit or nuts.

Very thin chocolate, such as cut-out shapes, stales quickly and therefore should not be kept long before using. However, because it is so thin and fragile it is advisable to keep it in the refrigerator. Providing it is left at room temperature to set and that it is stored in the refrigerator in a covered box and for as short a time as possible, there is little risk of it developing bloom.

Horns. Cream horn pans can be used as molds for chocolate horns. They are attractive as cake decorations, but may also be used as cups for cream, fruit, ice cream or a truffle mixture. Polish the inside of the cream horn pans with paper towels dusted with cornstarch, page 22, then pour in melted chocolate. Tilt the pan until evenly coated and let stand until set, then repeat the process to obtain a thicker layer of chocolate. Let stand until set hard, then carefully ease out of the pan.

Cups. Pour cooled melted chocolate into paper cups or petits four cups. Spread chocolate evenly inside the cups with a brush or spoon. Let stand until set, then add another layer of chocolate, if desired. Let stand until set hard, then peel away the paper cups. Fill larger ones with fruit and cream or mousse mixtures, smaller ones with nuts or truffle mixtures.

Shells. These make attractive containers for fruit, ice cream and sorbet. Cover scallop shells with plastic wrap, then brush with an even layer of chocolate. Let stand until hard, then carefully peel away plastic wrap.

Cutting chocolate shapes; preparing miniature chocolate cups.

Molding Chocolate

Simple molded chocolate decorations, colored chocolate shapes, page 24.

Chocolate molds made of aluminum or plastic are available in a wide variety of shapes and sizes. It is well worth making Easter eggs at home, and it is fun to experiment with different fillings for homemade chocolates.

Before using any chocolate molds, make sure they are absolutely clean and polish the insides with paper towels dusted with a little cornstarch; make sure all traces of cornstarch are removed before use. This preparation is vital to ensure that the chocolate will remove from the mold easily and that it has a shiny surface.

To make hollow shapes, pour melted chocolate into the mold, then tip the mold from side to side until evenly coated. Pour any excess chocolate back into the bowl. Place the molds hollow side down on waxed paper and let stand until set in a cool place (not the refrigerator). Large molds will require two or three coats of chocolate; allow each coat to set before adding the next.

When the chocolate is just beginning to set, gently scrape away any excess from around the rim of the mold. Once the chocolate is completely set, it shrinks away slightly from the mold and is easy to remove. Place the mold hollow-side down, tap gently all over and the chocolate will drop out easily. Use waxed paper when handling the chocolate, as warm hands will mark the surface.

Easter eggs. To make hollow shapes such as Easter eggs or rabbits, mold two halves and join them together. The easiest way to do this is to heat a baking sheet, then briefly touch the rim of each half against the hot metal. The chocolate will begin to melt and the two halves will seal when touched together. The seam will not be very obvious and can be disguised with piped icing. Decorations, such as eyes on rabbits and names on Easter eggs, can also be piped in icing. Ribbons make an attractive finish.

Homemade chocolates and sweets. Using sheets of chocolate molds, it is possible to produce a selection of im-

Easter eggs, molded from dark and white chocolate.

pressive homemade chocolates with a variety of fillings. Coat the molds with chocolate as for larger molds. When the chocolate is set, fill the cavity with chopped nuts, or a whole nut such as a hazelnut. Dried or glacé fruits which have been soaked in liqueur also make delicious fillings. Fondant centers and marzipan are equally suitable. Once the cavity has been filled, apply a final layer of chocolate to seal in the contents. Let stand until set, then remove from the mold.

Solid shapes are made simply by filling the mold with chocolate and letting set. Chocolate mice can be given a tail by holding a length of string in place before pouring the chocolate into the mold.

Special effects. A great variety of effects can be achieved by adding colors and flavorings to white chocolate before molding; special oil-based powder colors are available for this purpose. The desired quantity is stirred into the melted chocolate immediately before use.

The quantity of powder required to achieve bold colors, such as red and green, can affect the setting of white chocolate. More successful results can be obtained by using white chocolate flavored coating and molding buttons; these are available from specialist shops.

Colored animals are popular with children, and fruit shapes, colored appropriately, make attractive cake decorations. Christmas trees are easy to make using green coloring. It is possible to make a striking Father Christmas by using red for his clothes, leaving the fur and beard white, and using semisweet chocolate for his boots. Use the chocolate when it is fairly thick so that it will stay in position. Fill in one color at a time, letting each set before adding the next. These shapes can be used as a decoration for the Christmas tree or cake.

Specially formulated powder flavorings are also available. Like the powder colors, they are stirred (sparingly) into the melted chocolate. Fruit flavors are effective when added to colored fruit shapes, and mint or orange flavors combine well with dark chocolate.

Special effects with molding chocolate: Santa Claus and Christmas tree.

Selection of homemade chocolates with assorted fillings.

Coating with Chocolate

Coating fresh strawberries and grapes.

A wide variety of chocolate-coated sweets and petits four can be easily produced at home. Chocolate is easier to use for coating and dipping if one tablespoon vegetable oil is added for every eight ounces chocolate. The melted chocolate should be at 90F (32C) to 95F (35C) for coating. Pour the melted chocolate into a narrow container such as a jar or glass to give a good depth of chocolate. Hold whatever is to be coated on a dipping fork or cocktail stick, then dip it into the chocolate. Allow any excess chocolate to run off, then push the coated sweet or fruit off the fork or stick with another fork or cocktail stick onto waxed paper. Let stand in a cool place to set.

Peppermint creams, fudge, toffee, nut brittle, marzipan, fondant and truffles are delicious half or totally coated in chocolate.

Chocolate-coated fruits are simple but effective. Strawberries and grapes with their stalks intact look particularly attractive half coated, but many other fruits such as orange sections, kiwifruit and pineapple are suitable. Make sure fruits are clean and completely dry before dipping. Also try glacé, crystallized and candied fruits such as pineapple, ginger or strips of orange peel, but wash off the sugary coating and dry them thoroughly first.

Chocolate-coated cherries and marzipan-stuffed dates are delicious served with after-dinner coffee, and nuts such as walnuts and almonds are also enhanced by a chocolate coating.

Selection of chocolate-coated nuts, fresh fruit, candied peel, glacé fruit, truffles, fondants and stuffed dates.

Chocolate Zabaglione

1/3 cup sugar
1/4 cup rum
4 egg yolks
1 ounce semisweet chocolate, finely
  grated

To Serve:
Ladyfingers, opposite

Combine sugar, rum and egg yolks in a medium-size bowl. Set over a pan of gently simmering water and whisk until thick and mousse-like, 5 to 7 minutes. Fold in grated semisweet chocolate.

Pour into 4 glasses and serve immediately with lady fingers.

Makes 4 servings.

Ladyfingers: Preheat oven to 375F (190C). Line a baking sheet with parchment paper. In a large bowl set over a pan of hot water, whisk 3 tablespoons sugar and 1 egg until thick and mousse-like. Carefully fold in 1/4 cup sifted all-purpose flour.

Using a pastry bag fitted with a 1/2-inch plain nozzle, pipe finger lengths of mixture onto prepared baking sheet. Bake in preheated oven 6 to 8 minutes, until golden. Cool on a wire rack.

Note: This is a variation of the classic Italian marsala-flavored dessert. It must be served immediately, while still warm.

Italian Baked Peaches

3 ounces amaretti cookes (macaroons), coarsely crushed
1 ounce semisweet chocolate, finely grated
2 tablespoons unsalted butter, softened
4 large peaches
1 tablespoon sugar

Preheat oven to 375F (190C). Butter a shallow baking dish.

Combine cookie crumbs, grated chocolate and butter in a medium-size bowl.

Place peaches in a large bowl and cover with boiling water; let stand 1 minute. Transfer peaches to a large bowl filled with cold water; let stand 1 minute. Remove, carefully peel and cut in half. Discard pits. Using a teaspoon, scoop out a small amount of pulp from each peach half, chop and add to chocolate mixture.

Fill each peach half with chocolate filling, then sprinkle with sugar. Bake in preheated oven 30 minutes, until peaches are soft and filling is crisp. Serve hot.

Makes 4 servings.

Note: Although the peaches should not be too hard, over-ripe peaches should be avoided as they collapse during cooking.

Amaretti cookies are available in Italian delicatessens and some supermarkets. If unobtainable, use ratafia cookies instead.

Variations: As an alternative to amaretti cookies, ground almonds or hazelnuts may be used.

Either filling may also be used to stuff pears.

Strawberry-Chocolate Crepes

Crepes:
1 cup all-purpose flour
1 tablespoon unsweetened cocoa powder
1 tablespoon sugar
2 eggs, beaten
1-3/4 cups milk
2 tablespoons butter, melted
Additional butter for frying

Crème Pâtissière:
4 egg yolks
1/4 cup sugar
1/4 cup all-purpose flour
1-1/4 cups milk
1 vanilla bean

Filling:
32 to 36 strawberries, hulled, sliced

To Serve:
1 tablespoon Grand Marnier
1 tablespoon powdered sugar, sifted

To prepare crepes, sift flour and cocoa into a large bowl. Stir in sugar, then stir in beaten eggs. Gradually beat in milk and melted butter. Let batter stand at least 2 hours.

Rub bottom of a small skillet with a little butter and heat over medium heat. Pour in 2 tablespoons of batter. Cook about 1 minute on each side. Repeat with remaining batter.

Preheat oven to 350F (175C). To prepare crème pâtissière, in a medium-size bowl, mix egg yolks, sugar, flour and a small amount of milk. In a small saucepan, heat remaining milk and vanilla bean until almost boiling. Remove vanilla bean; pour milk into egg yolk mixture, stirring constantly. Return mixture to pan and cook gently, stirring constantly, 2 to 3 minutes.

Place 1 spoonful of crème pâtissière on a quarter of each crepe. Top with sliced strawberries. Fold crepe in a triangle, enclosing filling. Arrange crepes in a warmed buttered ovenproof dish. Cover with foil and heat in oven 10 to 12 minutes.

Warm Grand Marnier, ignite and pour over crepes. Dust with powdered sugar and serve.

Makes 16 to 18 crepes.

Chocolate Waffles

4 tablespoons butter
2 ounces semisweet chocolate
1-1/2 cups all-purpose flour
1 tablespoon baking powder
1 tablespoon plus 2 teaspoons sugar
2 eggs, separated
1-1/4 cups milk
Melted butter

To Serve:
Whipped cream, ground cinnamon
    and chocolate-dipped strawberries,
    if desired

Melt butter and chocolate, page 12; cool.

Sift flour and baking powder into a large bowl. Stir in sugar. Make a well in center; add egg yolks and mix thoroughly. Gradually add milk, alternating with chocolate and butter mixture. Beat thoroughly.

In a bowl, whisk egg whites until stiff but not dry. Fold egg whites gently into chocolate batter.

Brush a waffle iron with melted butter and heat until hot; set on medium heat. Pour in a small amount of batter and close waffle iron. Cook about 1 minute on each side or until both sides of waffle are crisp and golden-brown.

Do not stack waffles on top of each other or they will become soft very quickly.

Top with whipped cream, sprinkle with cinnamon and serve hot with strawberries, if desired.

Makes about 10 waffles.

Variation: For waffles with more chocolate flavor, substitute 2 tablespoons unsweetened cocoa powder for 2 tablespoons flour.

Chocolate Tagliatelle

Tagliatelle:
2 eggs
About 1-1/2 cups bread flour
2 tablespoons unsweetened cocoa
powder
2 tablespoons powdered sugar

Sauce:
2 ounces white chocolate
2/3 cup whipping cream

To Decorate:
Semisweet chocolate curls, if desired

To prepare tagliatelle, in a large bowl, beat eggs. Sift 1-1/2 cups flour, cocoa and powdered sugar over eggs. Mix with a fork, then press in a ball with hands. Dough should be firm but pliable and not sticky; add more flour if too moist. On a lightly floured surface, knead firmly 5 to 10 minutes or until smooth. Wrap in a damp towel and let rest 30 minutes.

Roll out dough on a lightly floured surface. Roll away from you, lifting and stretching dough as you roll, until very thin and smooth. Spread on a towel and let dry 30 minutes.

Loosely roll up pasta sheet in a cylinder. Using a sharp knife, cut in narrow strips. Spread over a towel placed over back of a chair, and let rest 20 minutes.

Fill a large saucepan with water; bring to a boil. Cook tagliatelle in boiling water 3 to 4 minutes or until just tender; drain thoroughly.

To prepare sauce, in a small saucepan, heat white chocolate and whipping cream over low heat, stirring constantly, until chocolate has melted and sauce is smooth.

Serve tagliatelle with sauce. Garnish with chocolate curls, if desired.

Makes 4 to 6 servings.

Note: A pasta machine may be used for rolling and cutting tagliatelle, if desired.

Chocolate Fondue

1 pineapple
1 mango
2 kiwifruit
1-3/4 cups strawberries
8 ounces seedless green grapes
2 or 3 figs

Fondue:
8 ounces semisweet chocolate, broken
  in pieces
2/3 cup whipping cream
2 tablespoons brandy

Peel and core pineapple; cut in cubes. Peel mango and slice. Peel kiwifruit and cut in wedges. Cut figs in quarters. Arrange all fruit on 6 individual plates and chill.

To prepare fondue, place chocolate and whipping cream into a fondue pot. Heat gently, stirring constantly, until chocolate has melted. Stir in brandy; beat until smooth.

Place fondue pot over a burner to keep warm. Serve fondue with fruit for dipping.

Makes 6 servings.

Variations: For children, substitute orange juice for brandy.

In addition to fruit for dipping, serve small cookies, sponge cakes or meringues. Almond Fingers, page 103, Ladyfingers, page 28, or meringues from Ginger & Chocolate Meringues, page 94, would be ideal.

Almond Fondue: Use Toblerone candy as an alternative to semisweet chocolate and substitute amaretto for brandy.

Mocha Fondue: Use coffee-flavored chocolate as an alternative to semisweet chocolate and add 3 tablespoons strong coffee. Use Kahlua or Tia Maria in place of brandy.

Orange Fondue: Add juice and grated peel of 1/2 orange to chocolate and whipping cream before melting chocolate. Use Grand Marnier in place of brandy.

Cranberry & Pecan Cake

Topping:
4 tablespoons unsalted butter
1/2 cup sugar
1 (12-oz.) package cranberries
1/2 cup coarsely chopped pecans

Cake:
3 eggs
1/3 cup sugar
2/3 cup self-rising flour
2 tablespoons unsweetened cocoa
  powder
Pinch of baking powder
1/2 teaspoon ground cinnamon
3 tablespoons unsalted butter, melted

Preheat oven to 350F (175C). Place a baking sheet in preheated oven.

To prepare topping, spread butter over bottom and side of a 9-inch round cake pan. Coat with sugar. In a bowl, mix cranberries and pecans; spread evenly over bottom of pan.

To prepare cake, in a bowl set over a pan of hot but not boiling water, whisk eggs and sugar until thick and light and whisk leaves a trail when lifted out of mixture. Sift flour, cocoa, baking powder and cinnamon into a bowl, then sift flour mixture, a small amount at a time, into egg mixture, folding in carefully each time. Fold in melted butter.

Pour cake mixture over topping. Place pan on heated baking sheet and bake in preheated oven 40 minutes or until cake is firm and a skewer inserted into center comes out clean.

Let cake cool in pan 10 minutes. Turn out onto a plate and cut in wedges to serve.

Makes 6 to 8 servings.

Note: This cake may be served hot or cold, but is particularly good served warm with whipped cream. It is best eaten on the day it is made.

Clafoutis aux Cerises et Chocolat

1 pound dark sweet cherries, pitted
1/4 cup plus 2 tablespoons sugar
3 eggs
1/2 cup self-rising flour
2 tablespoons unsweetened cocoa
   powder
2/3 cup whipping cream
1-1/4 cups milk
2 tablespoons kirsch

Chocolate Cream:
1-1/4 cups whipping cream
4 ounces semisweet chocolate, broken
   in pieces

To Decorate:
Powdered sugar

Preheat oven to 375F (190C). Lightly butter a 9-inch flan pan.

Arrange cherries in buttered pan; sprinkle with 2 tablespoons of sugar and set aside.

In a large bowl, whisk eggs and remaining sugar until light and frothy. Sift flour and cocoa onto a plate; add all at once to egg mixture and beat in thoroughly. Whisk in whipping cream, then milk and kirsch. Pour batter over cherries. Bake in preheated oven 50 to 60 minutes or until slightly risen and set in middle.

Meanwhile, prepare chocolate cream. In a small saucepan, heat whipping cream until almost boiling. Remove from heat and stir in chocolate until completely melted.

Sift powdered sugar over clafoutis. Serve warm with chocolate cream.

Makes 6 to 8 servings.

Variations: Plums, pears, apples or red or black currants may be used in place of cherries.

Rum Fudge Pudding

1/2 cup self-rising flour
1/4 cup unsweetened cocoa powder
6 tablespoons margarine, softened
1/3 cup granulated sugar
1 egg
2 tablespoons dark-brown sugar
1/2 cup chopped walnuts

Sauce:
1-1/4 cups hot coffee
2 tablespoons plus 2 teaspoons sugar
3 tablespoons rum

To Serve:
Sifted powdered sugar
Whipped cream

Preheat oven to 325F (160C). Grease a 5-cup ovenproof dish.

Sift flour and cocoa into a medium-size bowl. Add margarine, granulated sugar and egg and beat thoroughly about 2 minutes. Turn into greased dish and sprinkle with brown sugar and chopped walnuts.

To prepare sauce, in a small bowl, mix coffee, sugar and rum. Carefully pour over pudding.

Bake in preheated oven 50 to 60 minutes, until firm to touch in center. Sprinkle with powdered sugar and serve hot with whipped cream.

Makes 4 to 6 servings.

Chocolate Soufflés

3 tablespoons unsalted butter
1/3 cup all-purpose flour
1 cup milk
4 ounces semisweet chocolate,
**   chopped**
1 teaspoon instant coffee granules
1/4 cup sugar
3 eggs, separated, plus 1 egg white
2 tablespoons Tia Maria
Powdered sugar

Preheat oven to 375F (190C). Grease 10 individual ramekin dishes.

Melt butter in a medium-size saucepan over low heat. Remove from heat and blend in flour.

Gradually pour in milk, stirring until blended; return to heat. Bring to a boil, stirring constantly, and cook 3 minutes. Remove from heat and stir in chocolate, coffee granules and sugar; stir until chocolate melts. Stir in egg yolks and Tia Maria.

In a large bowl, whisk egg whites until fairly stiff. Using a metal spoon, fold 1/4 of whisked egg whites into chocolate mixture to lighten; carefully fold in remaining egg whites. Spoon into greased ramekins.

Bake in preheated oven 20 to 25 minutes, until well risen. Sprinkle with powdered sugar and serve at once.

Makes 10 soufflés.

Rich Chocolate Ice Cream

2 eggs plus 2 yolks
1/2 cup sugar
1-1/4 cups half and half
8 ounces semisweet chocolate,
chopped
1-1/4 cups whipping cream
1/4 cup dark rum

In a large bowl, combine eggs, yolks and sugar. In a large saucepan, heat half and half and chocolate gently until chocolate is melted. Stir well to blend, then bring to a boil, stirring constantly. Pour chocolate mixture onto egg mixture, stirring vigorously, then transfer to top of a double boiler or a bowl set over a pan of boiling water. Cook, stirring constantly, until custard is thick enough to coat back of spoon. Strain into a bowl and cool.

In a large bowl, whip whipping cream and rum until stiff, then fold into cooled chocolate mixture. Pour into a rigid freezerproof container. Cover, seal and freeze about 4 hours, until firm.

Scoop into chilled serving dishes to serve.

Makes 6 to 8 servings.

Chestnut & Orange Ice Cream

**1 (15-1/2-oz.) can unsweetened
  chestnut puree
2 eggs, separated
Finely grated peel and juice of 1
  orange
3 tablespoons Cointreau
2 tablespoons honey
1/2 cup sugar
2/3 cup water
1-1/4 cups whipping cream**

Chocolate Sauce:
**8 ounces semisweet chocolate,
  chopped
1/4 cup sugar
2/3 cup water**

To Decorate:
Shredded orange peel

In a blender or food processor fitted with the metal blade, process chestnut puree, egg yolks, orange peel and juice, Cointreau and honey until smooth.

In a large bowl, whisk egg whites until stiff, then whisk in sugar until glossy and thick. In a medium-size bowl, whip cream, then fold into whisked egg whites with chestnut mixture until thoroughly incorporated. Pour into a rigid freezer-proof container. Cover, seal and freeze 4 hours, until solid.

To prepare chocolate sauce, in a small saucepan, combine chocolate, sugar and water and heat gently, stirring frequently, until sugar is dissolved. Bring to a boil and simmer gently 5 minutes; cool.

Remove ice cream from freezer and let soften slightly, about 15 minutes. Using a melon baller, scoop ice cream in small balls and place on a baking sheet. Return to freezer about 30 minutes, until hard.

Pile ice cream balls into chilled serving dishes. Pour chocolate sauce over ice cream balls and decorate with shredded orange peel to serve.

Makes 8 servings.

Malibu Ice Cream

1/4 cup cream of coconut
2 eggs, separated
1/2 cup sugar
1-1/4 cups half and half
3 tablespoons Malibu liqueur
2/3 cup whipping cream
1 recipe Chocolate Sauce, page 39

In a large bowl, blend cream of coco-nut, egg yolks and 1/2 of sugar and beat well.

Reserve 2 tablespoons of half and half for decoration. In a small sauce-pan, bring remaining half and half to a boil, then pour onto egg yolk mix-ture, stirring vigorously. Return mix-ture to pan and cook over low heat until slightly thickened; cool. Stir in Malibu.

In a large bowl, whip whipping cream until it holds its shape.

In a small bowl, whisk egg whites until stiff, then whisk in remaining sugar. Fold whisked egg whites into whipped cream, then fold in coconut custard.

Pour into a rigid freezerproof con-tainer. Cover, seal and freeze about 4 hours, until firm.

Using a melon baller, scoop ice cream in small balls and place on a baking sheet. Return to freezer 1 hour, until hard. Meanwhile, prepare chocolate sauce.

Pour a pool of chocolate sauce onto each individual serving plate. Place small dots of reserved half and half at intervals on chocolate sauce. Using a skewer, swirl in an attractive design. Arrange ice cream balls in center and serve immediately.

Makes 6 servings.

Crème de Menthe Bombes

3 egg yolks
1/2 cup sugar
1-1/4 cups half and half
2 drops green food coloring
3 tablespoons crème de methe
1-1/4 cups whipping cream
4 ounces crisp chocolate mints,
  coarsely chopped

To serve:
1 recipe Chocolate Sauce, page 39
Frosted mint leaves, opposite

In a medium-size bowl, beat egg yolks and sugar until creamy. In a small saucepan, bring half and half to a boil, pour onto egg yolk mixture and mix well. Transfer to top of a double boiler or a bowl set over a pan of boiling water. Cook, stirring constantly, until thick enough to coat back of spoon. Strain into a bowl. Stir in food coloring and crème de menthe; cool.

In a large bowl, whip whipping cream until stiff, then whisk in mint custard. Pour into a rigid, freezer-proof container. Cover and freeze about 3 hours, until half set. Stir well and mix in chopped chocolate mints.

Spoon into 6 (2/3-cup) molds. Cover with foil and return to freezer until firm. Meanwhile, prepare chocolate sauce.

To serve, dip each mold into warm water to loosen ice cream and turn out onto a chilled plate. Pour chocolate sauce around each bombe and decorate with frosted mint leaves.

Makes 6 servings.

Frosted Mint Leaves: Brush leaves with egg whites, then dip into superfine sugar to coat. Set on waxed paper 1 to 2 hours to dry.

Chocolate-Vanilla Bombes

Chocolate Ice Cream:
1 egg plus 1 yolk
1/4 cup sugar
2/3 cup half and half
3 ounces semisweet chocolate, chopped
2/3 cup whipping cream
2 tablespoons dark rum

Vanilla Ice Cream:
1 egg white
1/4 cup sugar
1-1/4 cups whipping cream
1/2 teaspoon vanilla extract

To Serve:
1 recipe Chocolate Sauce, page 39
8 chocolate leaves, page 16

Prepare chocolate ice cream as for Rich Chocolate Ice Cream, page 38.

To prepare vanilla ice cream, in a small bowl, whisk egg white until stiff, then whisk in sugar. In a medium-size bowl, whip whipping cream until thick. Fold in whisked egg white and vanilla. Divide mixture among 8 individual 3/4-cup pudding molds; it will about half fill molds.

Spoon chocolate ice cream mixture over vanilla ice cream. Place molds on a baking sheet and freeze about 3 hours, until solid. Cover each mold with foil and seal and return to freezer until needed.

To serve, dip each mold into warm water and invert bombes onto chilled serving plates. Pour chocolate sauce around each bombe and decorate with a chocolate leaf.

Makes 8 servings.

Speckled Ice Cream

1-1/2 cups whole-wheat bread crumbs
1/4 cup packed light-brown sugar
1-1/4 cups whipping cream
3 egg whites
1/2 cup granulated sugar
**2 ounces semisweet chocolate,
   chopped or coarsely grated**

To Decorate:
Whipped cream
8 chocolate leaves, page 16

Preheat broiler.

In a flameproof dish, combine bread crumbs and brown sugar. Broil until golden-brown and crisp, stirring frequently; cool.

In a medium-size bowl, lightly whip whipping cream. In a large bowl, whisk egg whites until stiff; gradually whisk in granulated sugar. Fold whipped cream into whisked egg whites with bread-crumb mixture and chocolate.

Turn mixture into a 4-cup freezer-proof mold or bowl. Cover and freeze several hours, until firm.

To serve, invert mold or bowl over a plate. Wring out a towel in hot water and place over mold. When towel is cold, wring it out in hot water again and place over mold. Remove mold. If ice cream has melted on outside, return to freezer a few minutes.

To decorate, using a pastry bag fitted with a star nozzle, pipe whipped cream on each ice cream and top with a chocolate leaf.

Makes 8 servings.

Note: This ice cream does not freeze really solid, therefore it is possible to serve it straight from the freezer.

Frozen Praline Ring

Praline:
1/2 cup sugar
1/2 cup whole unblanched almonds

Chocolate Ice Cream:
6 ounces semisweet chocolate,
** chopped**
2/3 cup half and hlaf
1-1/4 cups whipping cream
2 tablespoons brandy

To Decorate:
Whipped cream

To prepare praline, oil a baking sheet. In a small, heavy-bottom saucepan, heat sugar and almonds gently until sugar is melted. Increase heat and cook until almonds begin to pop and turn brown, shaking pan to ensure almonds are evenly coated with caramel. Pour onto oiled baking sheet and let praline stand until hard.

To prepare chocolate ice cream, in a small pan, heat chocolate and half and half very gently until chocolate is melted. Stir until smooth; cool.

In a large bowl, whip whipping cream until it forms soft peaks. Carefully whisk in chocolate mixture and brandy; do not over-whip.

Crush praline with a rolling pin or in a food processor fitted with the metal blade. Reserve a small amount of praline for decoration. Fold remaining praline into chocolate mixture.

Spoon into a 3-1/3-cup ring mold. Cover with foil and freeze overnight.

To serve, turn mold upside down over a chilled plate. Rub mold with a cloth wrung out in very hot water, until ice cream drops out.

To decorate, using a pastry bag fitted with a star nozzle, pipe whipped cream around top of ice cream and sprinkle with reserved praline. Cut in slices to serve.

Makes 8 servings.

Chocolate & Brandy Bombe

Chocolate Ice Cream:
2 eggs plus 2 yolks
1/2 cup sugar
1-1/4 cups half and half
8 ounces semisweet chocolate,
  chopped
1-1/4 cups whipping cream
1/4 cup brandy

Filling:
3/4 cup whipping cream
1 tablespoon brandy
1 tablespoon powdered sugar
2 ounces meringues, broken in pieces

Prepare chocolate ice cream as for Rich Chocolate Ice Cream, page 38, adding brandy instead of rum. Freeze about 4 hours, until firm. Chill a 6-1/4-cup bombe mold or pudding bowl.

To prepare filling, in a medium-size bowl, whip whipping cream, brandy and powdered sugar until it stand in stiff peaks. Fold in meringues.

Reserve 1/4 cup chocolate ice cream. Line chilled mold or bowl thickly with remaining chocolate ice cream. Fill center with meringue cream and cover with reserved chocolate ice cream. Cover bombe or bowl with foil and freeze overnight.

To serve, dip mold or bowl in cold water to loosen bombe. Wipe a cloth around outside, then turn out onto a chilled plate. Cut in wedges to serve.

Makes 8 servings.

Note: Decorate with chocolate leaves, page 16, if desired.

Bombe aux Deux Chocolats

Dark Chocolate Ice Cream:
2 eggs plus 2 egg yolks
1/3 cup sugar
1-1/4 cups half and half
8 ounces semisweet chocolate,
 chopped
1-1/4 cups whipping cream

White Chocolate Ice Cream:
5 ounces white chocolate, chopped
2/3 cup milk
1/4 cup sugar
1-1/4 cups whipping cream

To Decorate:
Chocolate caraque, page 16

Place a 6-cup bombe mold in freezer.

To prepare dark chocolate ice cream, in a large bowl, beat eggs, egg yolks and sugar. In a medium-size saucepan, heat half and half and chocolate gently until chocolate is melted. Bring to a boil, then add to egg mixture. Stir until smooth. Strain into a bowl; cool.

In a medium-size bowl, whip whipping cream until thick but not too stiff; fold into chocolate mixture. Pour into a freezerproof container.

Cover and freeze 1 hour. Stir well, then refreeze until almost solid.

Line bombe mold with chocolate ice cream. Return to freezer.

To prepare white chocolate ice cream, in a small saucepan, gently heat chocolate and 1/2 of milk until milk is warm and chocolate is beginning to melt. Turn off heat. Stir gently until chocolate has melted completely; set aside.

In a large saucepan, heat sugar and remaining milk; cool.

Stir melted chocolate mixture into sweetened milk. In a medium-size bowl, whip whipping cream until thick but not stiff; fold gently into chocolate mixture. Fill center of bombe with white chocolate mixture. Cover and freeze several hours, until firm.

To serve, dip mold into cold water. Turn out onto a chilled serving dish and decorate with caraque.

Makes 6 to 8 servings.

Ratafia Tortoni

2 egg whites
1/3 cup powdered sugar
2/3 cup half and half
1-3/4 cups whipping cream
3 tablespoons medium-dry sherry
4 ounces ratafias or amaretti cookies
   (macaroons), crushed
2 ounces semisweet chocolate, grated

To Decorate:
8 ratafias (macaroons)
Whipped cream

In a large bowl, whisk egg whites until stiff, then gradually whisk in powdered sugar. In another large bowl, whisk half and half, whipping cream and sherry until soft peaks form. Fold in whisked egg whites.

Reserve 1/4 cup of crushed cookies. Gently fold remaining crushed cookies into cream mixture with grated chocolate. Pour into an 8" x 4" loaf pan. Freeze uncovered until ice cream is frozen around edges; stir with a fork until a creamy consistency. Return to freezer and freeze several hours, until firm.

Transfer to refrigerator 30 minutes before serving to soften slightly. Turn out of pan. Press reserved crushed cookies over top and sides of tortoni. Decorate with ratafias, securing them with whipping cream. Cut in slices to serve.

Makes 8 servings.

Note: Although this ice cream is traditionally made in a loaf shape, it may also be frozen in a bombe mold or bowl. The crumb coating may be omitted, if desired.

Variations: Combine nuts with crushed cookies and substitute brandy or rum for sherry.

Frozen Vanilla Slice

Chocolate Cake:
2 eggs
1/3 cup sugar
1/2 cup all-purpose flour, sifted
3 tablespoons unsweetened cocoa
   powder, sifted

Vanilla Ice:
1 egg white
1/4 cup sugar
1 cup whipping cream
1/4 teaspoon vanilla extract

To Finish:
3 tablespoons crème de cacao
3 tablespoons cold coffee

To Serve:
1 recipe Chocolate Sauce, page 39

Preheat oven to 375F (190C). Grease and flour a baking sheet and mark a 13" x 8" rectangle.

Prepare cake as for Strawberry Gâteau, page 76. Spread mixture onto marked rectangle on prepared baking sheet. Bake in preheated oven 8 minutes.

To prepare vanilla ice, in a medium-size bowl, whisk egg white until stiff. Whisk in sugar. In a small bowl, whip whipping cream with vanilla until thick; fold into whisked egg white.

Line an 8" x 4" loaf pan with waxed paper. Cut cake in 3 equal strips. Lay 1 piece in lined loaf pan, trimming to fit.

In a glass measure, combine crème de cacao and coffee and sprinkle a small amount over cake. Spread 1/2 of vanilla mixture over top. Place another piece of cake on top, trim to fit and sprinkle with remaining coffee mixture. Spread with remaining vanilla ice. Top with remaining piece of cake and trim. Press down gently, cover with foil and freeze until solid. Meanwhile, prepare chocolate sauce.

To serve, dip pan into warm water to loosen frozen dessert, then turn out onto a flat surface. Slice with a sharp knife and place slices on chilled individual serving plates. Spoon chocolate sauce over dessert to serve.

Makes 8 servings.

Chocolate-Chestnut Dessert

Cake:
1/3 cup sugar
2 eggs
1/2 cup all-purpose flour, sifted

Chocolate & Chestnut Ice:
8 ounces semisweet chocolate, chopped
1 tablespoon plus 2 teaspoons superfine sugar
2/3 cup half and half
1 (15-1/2-oz.) can unsweetened chestnut puree
1/4 cup brandy
1-1/4 cups whipping cream

To Decorate:
Whipped cream
Grated semisweet chocolate

Preheat oven to 375F (190C). Grease and flour 4 baking sheets and mark an 8-inch circle on each.

Prepare cake as for Chocolate Zuppe Inglese, page 69. Spread mixture evenly over circles. Bake in preheated oven, 2 at a time, 6 to 8 minutes until golden-brown. Using a palette knife, remove from baking sheets and trim each to an 8-inch round.

To prepare Chocolate & Chestnut Ice, in a small saucepan, gently heat chocolate, sugar and half and half until chocolate is melted. In a blender or food processor fitted with the metal blade, process chocolate mixture, chestnut puree and brandy until smooth. Pour into a large bowl and chill. In a medium-size bowl, whip whipping cream until thick, then fold in chestnut mixture.

Lay a cake round in bottom of a deep 8-inch loose-bottom cake pan. Spoon 1/4 of chestnut mixture over cake round and press down firmly so that mixture runs down side of cake round to give a chocolate edge. Place a second cake round on top. Repeat layers, finishing with chestnut mixture. Cover with foil and freeze until solid.

Remove frozen dessert from pan. Decorate with piped whipped cream and grated chocolate. Place in refrigerator 30 minutes before serving to soften. Cut in wedges to serve.

Makes 10 servings.

Frozen Chocolate-Orange Dessert

Chocolate Cake:
2 eggs
1/3 cup sugar
1/2 cup all-purpose flour
1 tablespoon unsweetened cocoa
  powder

Orange Ice Cream:
Grated peel and juice of 2 oranges
3 eggs, separated
2/3 cup sugar
1-1/4 cups whipping cream

To Serve:
1/4 cup Cointreau
1 ounce semisweet chocolate, melted,
  page 12

Preheat oven to 375F (190C). Line a deep 8-inch round cake pan with greased waxed paper. Dust with flour.

Prepare cake as for Strawberry Gâteau, page 76. Pour into prepared pan and bake in preheated oven 25 to 30 minutes, until cake springs back when lightly pressed. Turn out on a wire rack to cool.

To prepare ice cream, in a small bowl, beat orange peel, egg yolks and 1/2 of sugar using an electric mixer

until smooth. In another small bowl, whisk egg whites until stiff, then whisk in remaining sugar until thick and glossy.

Whip whipping cream until thick, then whisk in all but 1/4 cup of orange juice. Fold in egg yolk mixture, then fold into whisked egg whites.

Mix reserved orange juice with Cointreau. Split cake in half horizontally; put bottom half in clean cake pan and sprinkle with 1/2 of Cointreau mixture.

Spoon 1/2 of ice cream mixture over top; cover with remaining cake half. Press down firmly so mixture runs down side of cake. Sprinkle with remaining Cointreau mixture. Pour remaining ice cream mixture over cake. Cover with foil and chill overnight.

To serve, dip pan into warm water to loosen frozen dessert and turn out onto a chilled serving plate.

Using a pastry bag fitted with a writing nozzle, drizzle melted chocolate lines over top of dessert.

Makes 10 servings.

Frozen Mocha Soufflés

4 eggs, separated
3/4 cup powdered sugar, sifted
3 ounces semisweet chocolate,
   chopped
1 tablespoon instant coffee granules
2 tablespoons water
1-1/4 cups whipping cream
2 tablespoons Kahlua

To Decorate:
Grated semisweet chocolate

Place a double band of foil very tightly around 6 ramekin dishes to stand 1 inch above rim of dishes.

In a large bowl, beat egg yolks and powdered sugar using an electric mixer until very thick and mousse-like.

In a small saucepan, gently heat chocolate, coffee granules and water until chocolate is melted. Cool slightly, then whisk into egg yolk mixture.

In a medium-size bowl, whip whipping cream with Kahlua; set aside. In another medium-size bowl, whisk egg whites until stiff, then carefully fold into chocolate mixture with 3/4 of whipped cream. Pour into prepared ramekins and freeze overnight.

Remove foil carefully and, using a pastry bag fitted with a star nozzle, pipe remaining whipped cream around edge of each soufflé.

Decorate with grated chocolate and serve immediately.

Makes 6 servings.

Chocolate Brandy Creams

3 ounces semisweet chocolate,
  chopped
2/3 cup half and half
1-1/4 cups whipping cream
1 tablespoon powdered sugar, sifted
2 tablespoons brandy

To Decorate:
Chocolate curls, page 16

To Serve:
Almond Curls, opposite

In a small saucepan, very gently heat chocolate and half and half until chocolate is melted. Stir until smooth; cool.

In a medium-size bowl, whip whipping cream until thick, then carefully whisk in powdered sugar, brandy and chocolate mixture, taking care not to over-whip.

Spoon into 6 tall glasses and decorate with chocolate curls. Chill until required. Serve with Almond Curls.

Makes 6 servings.

Almond Curls: Preheat oven to 400F (205C). Grease and flour 2 baking sheets. In a medium-size bowl, mix 1/4 cup sifted all-purpose flour with 1/4 cup sugar. Make a well in center and add 1 egg white and 2 tablespoons melted butter; mix until smooth.

Drop teaspoonfuls of mixture onto prepared baking sheets. Spread in 2-1/2-inch circles and sprinkle with 2 tablespoons sliced almonds.

Bake in preheated oven 6 to 7 minutes, until pale-golden. Remove with a palette knife and curl around handle of a wooden spoon. Let stand until firm, then remove.

St. Emilion Dessert

1 tablespoon brandy
1 tablespoon Amaretto liqueur
6 ounces ratafia cookies (macaroons)
8 tablespoons unsalted butter,
  softened
1/2 cup sugar
8 ounces semisweet chocolate, melted,
  page 12
1-1/4 cups milk
2 eggs, beaten

To Decorate:
Whipped cream
Chocolate leaves, page 16

In a small bowl, mix brandy and Amaretto. Arrange a layer of cookies in a glass bowl. Sprinkle with 1/2 of brandy mixture. Place remaining cookies on a plate and sprinkle with remaining brandy mixture.

In a medium-size bowl, cream butter and sugar until light and fluffy. Stir in melted chocolate. In a medium-size saucepan, heat milk until almost boiling. Stir into beaten eggs; return mixture to pan. Stir over gentle heat until mixture thickens and coats back of spoon. Stir slowly into chocolate mixture. Chill until just beginning to set.

Spoon 1/2 of chocolate mixture over cookies in dish. Arrange soaked cookies on top. Cover with remaining chocolate mixture. Chill several hours or overnight.

Using a pastry bag fitted with a star nozzle, pipe whipped cream on dessert and decorate with chocolate leaves.

Makes 6 to 8 servings.

Note: This dessert looks most attractive prepared in individual dishes.

Variation: Amaretti cookies may be used in place of ratafias for a more pronounced almond flavor.

Zuccotto

3/4 cup plus 2 tablespoons self-rising
  flour
2 tablespoons unsweetened cocoa
  powder
1/2 teaspoon baking powder
1/2 cup sugar
8 tablespoons margarine, softened
2 eggs
3 tablespoons brandy
3 tablespoons cherry brandy

Filling:
1-1/4 cups whipping cream
2 tablespoons powdered sugar, sifted
1/2 cup chopped hazelnuts, toasted
8 ounces dark sweet cherries, pitted
2 ounces semisweet chocolate, grated
  or finely chopped

To Decorate:
1 tablespoon unsweetened cocoa
  powder
1 tablespoon powdered sugar

Preheat oven to 375F (190C). Grease a jellyroll pan and line with parchment paper.

Sift flour, cocoa and baking powder into a large bowl. Add sugar, margarine and eggs. Beat thoroughly until well mixed; pour into prepared pan. Bake in preheated oven 15 to 20 minutes or until well risen and firm to touch. Turn out onto a wire rack to cool.

Using rim of a 5-cup pudding bowl as a guide, cut a circle from cake. Line bowl with plastic wrap, then with remaining cake, cutting as necessary to fit.

In a small bowl, mix brandy and cherry brandy. Sprinkle over cake in bowl and cake round.

To prepare filling, in a medium-size bowl, whip whipping cream and powdered sugar until stiff. Fold in hazelnuts, cherries and chocolate.

Fill cake-lined bowl with cream mixture. Press cake round on top. Cover with a plate and a weight. Chill several hours or overnight.

Turn out onto a serving plate. Decorate with cocoa and powdered sugar, sifted over top.

Makes 6 servings.

Chocolate Christmas Pudding

1/3 cup glacé pineapple, coarsely
  chopped
1/3 cup chopped glacé cherries
1/3 cup raisins
Peel of 1/2 orange, if desired
3 tablespoons brandy
3 tablespoons half and half
12 ounces semisweet chocolate,
  chopped
1/2 cup cream cheese, softened
4 ounces ratafia cookies (macaroons),
  broken in pieces

To Serve:
Whipped cream
Grated semisweet chocolate

Grease a 3-3/4-cup pudding bowl.

In a small bowl, combine pineapple, cherries, raisins and orange peel, if desired. Pour brandy over fruit.

In a medium-size saucepan, very gently heat half and half and chocolate until melted. Stir until smooth. Add fruit with brandy; cool.

In a large bowl, beat cream cheese with a small amount of chocolate mixture until smooth, then beat in remaining chocolate mixture. Mix in cookies and pour into greased pudding bowl. Chill overnight.

To serve, turn out onto a chilled plate. Spoon some of whipped cream over pudding and let it trickle down sides; serve remaining whipped cream separately. Sprinkle pudding with grated chocolate.

Makes 10 to 12 servings.

Note: This pudding is extremely rich. Serve it cut in thin slices.

Steamed Chocolate Pudding

8 tablespoons unsalted butter,
  softened
1/2 cup sugar
1/2 teaspoon ground cinnamon
4 eggs, separated
4 ounces semisweet chocolate, melted,
  page 12, cooled
1 tablespoon brandy
2/3 cup whipping cream
1/4 cup crème fraîche

Lightly oil a 3-3/4 cup pudding bowl.
Pour enough water into a large deep
saucepan to come 1/3 of way up side
of bowl; bring to a boil.

In a large bowl, cream butter, sugar
and cinnamon until pale and thick.
Beat in egg yolks, 1 at a time. Carefully stir in cooled melted chocolate and
brandy.

In another large bowl, whisk egg
whites until stiff. Stir a small amount
of egg whites into chocolate mixture;
carefully fold in remaining egg
whites. Spoon chocolate mixture into

oiled bowl. Cover with oiled foil and
tie securely with string. Place bowl in
pan of boiling water. Cover pan and
simmer gently 45 minutes.

Let pudding stand in bowl until
completely cold; turn out onto serving dish.

In a small bowl, whisk whipping
cream and crème fraîche. Decorate
pudding with whipped-cream mixture or serve separately, if desired.

Makes 4 to 6 servings.

Note: The pudding will sink slightly
when removed from heat. This is
quite normal and contributes to the
rather dense, rich texture.

Variation: Cook in individual pudding molds 25 to 30 minutes. Remove
and decorate with piped whipped
cream mixture and chocolate hearts.

Raspberry-Chocolate Brûlées

8 ounces fresh raspberries or
  strawberries
2 tablespoons Framboise or
  strawberry liqueur
2 cups whipping cream
4 ounces semisweet chocolate, melted,
  page 12, cooled
1/2 cup packed light-brown sugar

To Decorate:
Mint leaves
12 to 16 fresh raspberries or
  strawberries

Spread raspberries or strawberries over bottom of 6 to 8 (2/3-cup) freezerproof ramekin dishes. Sprinkle with Framboise.

In a large bowl, whip whipping cream until it begins to hold its shape. Add cooled chocolate and continue whipping until cream is stiff. Spread over raspberries. Place in freezer until cream is frozen.

Preheat broiler. Sprinkle brown sugar thickly over cream. Broil until sugar is melted and caramelized.

Refrigerate brûlées until fruit and cream have thawed. Serve same day, decorated with mint leaves and fresh rasperries or strawberries.

Makes 6 to 8 servings.

Note: If you are short of time, it is not necessary to freeze brûlées before broiling, but it does prevent cream from bubbling up through sugar during broiling.

Always ensure broiler is preheated before broiling brûlées to caramelize brown sugar.

Variation: Use red currants or sliced peaches instead of raspberries or strawberries. Fresh fruit gives a better result than frozen.

Chocolate Terrine

White Chocolate Mousse:
2/3 cup whipping cream
2 eggs, separated
2 tablespoons sugar
4 ounces white chocolate, melted,
    page 12, cooled
1 (1/4-oz.) envelope unflavored gelatin
    (about 1 tablespoon) dissolved in 3
    tablespoons water

Dark Chocolate Mousse:
2/3 cup whipping cream
2 eggs, separated
1 tablespoon plus 2 teaspoons sugar
4 ounces semisweet chocolate, melted,
    page 12, cooled
1 (1/4-oz.) envelope unflavored
    gelatin, (about 1 tablespoon)
    dissolved in 3 tablespoons water

Orange Cream:
2 tablespoons sugar
1 tablespoon cornstarch
2/3 cup milk
2 egg yolks, lightly beaten
1 tablespoon Cointreau
1/4 cup frozen thawed orange juice
    concentrate
2/3 cup whipping cream

To Decorate:
Chocolate-dipped orange sections,
    page 26

To prepare white chocolate mousse, in a small bowl, whip whipping cream. In another small bowl, whisk egg whites until fairly stiff. In a third bowl, whisk egg yolks with sugar until thick and pale. Stir in cooled chocolate, then gelatin and then whipped cream. Gently fold in whisked egg whites. Pour mixture into an oiled 8" x 4" loaf pan. Freeze until firm.

Prepare dark chocolate mousse in same way. Pour over white chocolate mousse. Chill 2 hours or until set.

To prepare orange cream, in a saucepan, combine sugar, cornstarch and 2 tablespoons of milk; stir in remaining milk. Cook over low heat until thickened, stirring. Whisk egg yolks into mixture; cool. Stir in Cointreau, orange juice and cream.

Turn out terrine. Serve in slices, surrounded by orange cream. Decorate with chocolate orange sections.

Makes 6 to 8 servings.

Coeurs à la Crème au Chocolat

1 cup cottage cheese or ricotta cheese
1/3 cup powdered sugar, sifted
1-1/4 cups whipping cream
2 ounces semisweet chocolate, grated
2 egg whites

Chocolate Cream Sauce:
2/3 cup half and half
2 ounces semisweet chocolate, melted,
   page 12

Line 8 individual coeurs à la crème molds with muslin. Or line a sieve with muslin.

Press cheese through a sieve into a large bowl. Add powdered sugar and whipping cream and beat thoroughly. Stir in grated chocolate.

In a small bowl, whisk egg whites until stiff but not dry. Lightly fold into cheese mixture.

Spoon mixture into molds or prepared sieve. Refrigerate overnight to drain.

To prepare chocolate cream sauce, in a small bowl, pour 1/4 of half and half. Stir in melted chocolate. Reserve 1 tablespoon of remaining half and half. Gradually stir remaining half and half into chocolate mixture; stir until smooth.

Turn out each coeur à la crème onto a plate and pour chocolate cream around it. To decorate, drop dots of reserved half and half onto sauce and, using a skewer, feather in a design. If crème has been made in sieve, turn onto a serving dish and serve chocolate cream separately.

Makes 8 servings.

Variation: Coeurs à la crème may be served with fruit, such as raspberries or strawberries, or with fruit puree as a sauce instead of chocolate cream.

Chocolate-Orange Cups

8 ounces semisweet chocolate,
  chopped
1-1/4 cups half and half
Grated peel of 1 satsuma
2 tablespoon brandy
2 tablespoons whipping cream

In a medium-size saucepan, very gently heat chocolate, 1/2 of half and half and grated satsuma peel, stirring constantly, until chocolate is melted.

Stir in remaining half and half and brandy and pour into 6 cups or small ramekins.

In a pastry bag fitted with a writing nozzle, pipe a continuous whirl of whipping cream from center to edge of chocolate cups. Using a skewer, make a feathered design. Chill 2 to 3 hours until set.

Makes 4 to 6 servings.

Note: Do not allow chocolate mixture to set before piping whipping cream or you will not be able to create a feathered effect.

This is an extremely rich dessert, so only small portions are served.

White Chocolate Mousse

2/3 cup whipping cream
2 egg whites
3 tablespoons unsalted butter,
  softened
6 ounces white chocolate, melted,
  page 12
1 teaspoon triple-strength rose water
4 ounces semisweet chocolate, melted,
  page 12, cooled

To Decorate:
Crystallized rose petals, opposite

In a small bowl, whip whipping cream until thick, but not stiff. In another small bowl, whisk egg whites until stiff but not dry. Set both aside.

In a large bowl, beat butter into melted white chocolate until smooth and creamy. Cool but do not let set. Gently fold in whipped cream. Stir in rose water, then fold in whisked egg whites.

Spoon mixture into 6 (2/3-cup) ramekins or cups. Cover and chill until set.

Spread cooled melted semisweet chocolate evenly over mousses. Decorate with crystallized rose petals. Refrigerate until chocolate has hardened before serving.

Makes 6 servings.

Crystallized Rose Petals: Brush dry rose petals with egg white, dip into superfine sugar and set on waxed paper to dry. Store in an airtight container up to 3 days until needed.

If desired, use other flower petals. Crystallized violets and primroses are particularly attractive.

Variation: Mousses can be made with semisweet chocolate, flavored with rum or brandy instead of rose water and topped with a layer of white chocolate.

Chocolate-Strawberry Cones

3 tablespoons all-purpose flour
1 tablespoon unsweetened cocoa
   powder
1/4 cup sugar
1 egg white
2 tablespoons unsalted butter, melted
2 tablespoons chopped pistachios

Filling:
1 cup whipping cream
2 tablespoons Framboise
4 ounces strawberries, hulled

Preheat oven to 400F (205C). Grease and flour 3 baking sheets.

Sift flour and cocoa into a medium-size bowl; stir in sugar. Make a well in center. Add egg white and butter and beat until smooth. Place spoonfuls of mixture onto prepared baking sheets, spacing well apart, and spread out thinly to 4-inch circles. Sprinkle with nuts.

Bake in preheated oven 4 to 6 minutes. Remove with a palette knife and curl each around a cornet mold, holding in position until set. Remove from molds.

To prepare filling, in a small bowl, whip whipping cream and Framboise until thick. Spoon 1/4 of whipped cream into a pastry bag fitted with a large fluted nozzle.

Slice strawberries and reserve 12 slices. Fold remaining strawberry slices into remaining whipped cream and spoon into chocolate cones. Pipe a rosette of whipped cream on each and decorate with a strawberry slice.

Makes 12 cones.

Note: This mixture makes 15 cones, which allows for 3 breakages. Only bake 3 circles at a time or they will begin to set before you have time to roll them up.

Chocolate Brandy Snap Baskets

Brandy Snaps:
2 tablespoons unsalted butter or
   margarine
1/4 cup packed light-brown sugar
2 tablespoons corn syrup
1/2 cup all-purpose flour, sifted
6 ounces semisweet chocolate, melted,
   page 12

Filling:
1 egg white
1 tablespoon plus 2 teaspoons
   superfine sugar
2/3 cup whipping cream
2 tablespoons Framboise
4 ounces raspberries

Preheat oven to 350F (175C).

To prepare brandy snaps, in a small saucepan, gently heat butter or margarine, brown sugar and corn syrup until fat has melted and sugar is dissolved. Cool slightly, then beat in flour.

Drop 12 teaspoonfuls of mixture on 3 baking sheets, spacing well apart, and press out with wet fingertips in 5-inch circles. Bake in preheated oven, 1 sheet at a time, 7 to 10 minutes, until golden.

Cool slightly, then remove. Invert over bottom of an inverted glass; mold cookies to give wavy edges. Let stand a few minutes to set, then remove carefully. If cookies become too brittle to handle, return to oven 30 seconds to soften.

Place 1 spoonful of melted chocolate inside 1 basket and rotate to coat inside, using back of a teaspoon to help. Repeat with remaining chocolate and baskets; let stand until set.

To prepare filling, in a small bowl, whisk egg white until stiff, then whisk in sugar. In a separate bowl, whip cream and liqueur until thick. Fold in whisked egg white and all but 8 raspberries.

Spoon filling into baskets and decorate with reserved raspberries.

Makes 8 baskets.

Note: Cookie mixture will make 10 baskets, which allows for 2 breakages.

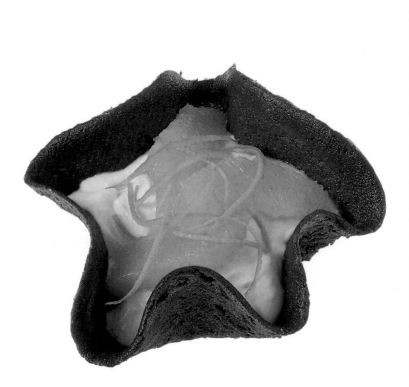

Cointreau Cream in Tulips

3 tablespoons all-purpose flour
1 tablespoon unsweetened cocoa
  powder
1/4 cup sugar
1 egg white
2 tablespoons unsalted butter, melted

Filling:
2 oranges
1 cup cottage cheese
2 tablespoons honey
2 tablespoons Cointreau
2/3 cup whipping cream

Preheat oven to 400F (205C). Grease and flour 3 baking sheets.

Sift flour and cocoa into a medium-size bowl; stir in sugar. Make a well in center. Add egg white and butter and beat until smooth. Drop spoonfuls of mixture onto prepared baking sheets and spread out thinly in 4-inch circles. Bake in preheated oven 4 to 6 minutes.

Remove from baking sheets and place each cookie, top-side down, over bottom of an inverted glass.

Mold cookie to give wavy edges. Let stand until hard, then carefully remove cookie.

To prepare filling, pare 2 strips of peel from 1 orange. Cut in needle-fine shreds and blanch in boiling water 1 minute. Drain on paper towels and set aside.

Finely grate peel from other orange. Peel and section both oranges, discarding all pith and seeds.

In a medium-size bowl, combine cottage cheese, honey, grated orange peel and Cointreau. In another bowl, whip cream until soft peaks form, then fold into cheese mixture.

Spoon filling into 6 tulip cups and decorate with orange sections and orange shreds.

Makes 6 servings.

Note: Cookies mixture will make 9 tulips, which allows for 3 breakages.

Chocolate Meringue Nests

1 tablespoon unsweetened cocoa
  powder
1/2 cup sugar
2 egg whites

Filling:
1/2 cup whipping cream
2 tablespoons crème de cacao
6 chocolate hearts, page 20

Preheat oven to 275F (135C). Line a baking sheet with parchment paper and mark 8 (3-inch) circles on it.

Sift cocoa and 1 tablespoon of sugar together; set aside.

In a small bowl, whisk egg whites until stiff and dry-looking. Gradually whisk in remaining sugar, until thick and glossy, then carefully fold in cocoa mixture. Using a pastry bag fitted with a 1/4-inch-fluted nozzle, pipe over each circle, starting from the center and working to edge, forming a bottom. Pipe on top of outside edge, forming a nest.

Bake in preheated oven 1-1/2 hours, until dry; cool.

In a small bowl, whip whipping cream and crème de cacao until thick. Spoon flavored cream into each meringue nest and decorate with chocolate hearts.

Makes 8 nests.

Hazelnut Galette with Kumquats

1 pound kumquats, halved lengthwise
3/4 cup sugar
1-1/4 cups water
2/3 cup whipping cream

Pastry:
6 tablespoons butter, softened
1/4 cup sugar
3/4 cup all-purpose flour
1/4 cup unsweetened cocoa powder
3/4 cup ground hazelnuts

To Decorate:
Powdered sugar

Preheat oven to 375F (190C).

Place kumquats in a large saucepan with sugar and water. Bring to a boil, then simmer gently 30 minutes. Drain and cool.

Meanwhile, prepare pastry in a large bowl, cream butter and sugar until light and fluffy. Sift in flour and cocoa. Add ground hazelnuts and mix thoroughly to make a firm dough.

Knead lightly on a floured surface until smooth. Divide dough in half and roll each piece to an 8-inch round on a baking sheet. Bake in preheated oven 15 to 20 minutes or until firm. Cut 1 round in 8 wedges while still warm. Transfer remaining round and wedges to wire racks to cool. In a small bowl, whip whipping cream and spread 3/4 of whipped cream over hazelnut round. Reserve 3 kumquats; arrange remainder on whipped cream. Place hazelnut wedges on top and sift powdered sugar over wedges. Using a pastry bag fitted with a star nozzle, pipe a rosette of remaining whipped cream on each wedge. Cut reserved kumquats in pieces and place a piece on each rosette. Serve immediately.

Makes 8 servings.

Variation: To prepare individual galettes, cut rolled out pastry in 8 (3-inch) rounds for bottoms and 8 (2-inch) rounds for tops. Bake 12 to 15 minutes. Assemble as above.

Profiteroles with Liqueur Cream

Choux Pastry:
4 tablespoons unsalted butter or margarine
2/3 cup water
1/3 cup all-purpose flour, sifted
2 eggs

Filling:
3/4 cup whipping cream
2 tablespoons crème de cacao

To Serve:
1 recipe Chocolate Sauce, page 39

Preheat oven to 425F (220C).

In a large pan, melt butter or margarine. Add water and bring to a boil. Add flour, all at once, and beat thoroughly until mixture leaves side of pan. Cool slightly, then vigorously beat in eggs, 1 at a time.

In a pastry bag fitted with a plain 1/2-inch nozzle, pipe small mounds of pastry onto a dampened baking sheet. Bake in preheated oven 10 minutes. Reduce temperature to 375F (190C) and bake 20 to 25 minutes more, until golden. Make a slit in side of each profiterole and cool on a wire rack.

To prepare filling, in a small bowl, whip whipping cream and crème de cacao until thick. In a pastry bag fitted with a 1/8-inch plain nozzle, pipe filling into each profiterole.

Pile profiteroles in pyramids on individual serving dishes. Pour chocolate sauce over profiteroles just before serving.

Makes 6 servings.

Chocolate-Chestnut Tart

8 ounces gingersnap cookies, crushed
6 tablespoons butter, melted

Filling:
3/4 cup unsweetened chestnut puree
1/4 cup sugar
Few drops vanilla extract
3/4 cup ricotta cheese
2 eggs
3-1/2 ounces semisweet chocolate,
**   melted, page 12**
1/4 cup ground almonds

To Decorate:
2/3 cup whipping cream, whipped
Chocolate shapes, page 20

Preheat oven to 350F (175C).

In a small bowl, combine cookie crumbs and melted butter. Press onto bottom and up side of a 9-inch loose-bottom flan pan. Bake in preheated oven 10 minutes; cool.

To prepare filling, in a small bowl, beat chestnut puree, sugar and vanilla until smooth.

In a medium-size bowl, beat ricotta cheese and eggs until smooth. Stir melted chocolate into cheese mixture. Add chestnut puree mixture and mix thoroughly. Stir in ground almonds.

Pour filling into prepared crust and bake in preheated oven 35 minutes or until lightly set. Cool, then chill thoroughly.

To decorate, spread a thin layer of whipped cream over top and sprinkle with grated chocolate. Using a pastry bag fitted with a star nozzle, pipe remaining whipped cream around edge and decorate with chocolate diamonds. Serve immediately.

Makes 6 to 8 servings.

Note: If unsweetened chestnut puree is unavailable, the sweetened version may be used. Omit sugar and vanilla from recipe, as sweetened chestnut puree usually tastes quite strongly of vanilla, and expect a sweeter result.

Chocolate Zuppe Inglese

Cake:
1/3 cup sugar
2 eggs
1/2 cup all-purpose flour, sifted

Chocolate Filling:
3 ounces semisweet chocolate, chopped
3 tablespoons milk
2/3 cup whipping cream

To Finish:
2/3 cup Marsala all'uova wine
2/3 cup whipping cream
Chocolate caraque, page 16
Powdered sugar

Preheat oven to 350F (175C). Grease a deep 8-inch round cake pan and line with waxed paper.

To prepare cake, in a medium-size bowl, beat sugar and eggs using an electric mixer until very thick and mousse-like and mixture leaves a trail when beaters are lifted. Carefully fold in flour. Spoon mixture into prepared pan and bake in preheated oven 20 to 25 minutes, until cake springs back when pressed lightly in center. Turn out onto a wire rack to cool.

To prepare filling, in a small saucepan, heat chocolate and milk very gently, stirring until chocolate is melted; cool. In a medium-size bowl, whip whipping cream and melted chocolate until it holds its shape.

Cut cake horizontally in 3 layers. Lay 1 layer on a serving plate. Pour 1/3 of wine over layer, then cover with 1/2 of filling. Repeat cake and filling layers, pouring remaining wine over top layer of cake.

To finish, in a small bowl, whip whipping cream until fairly thick; spread over top and side of filled cake. Decorate with chocolate caraque and sprinkle with powdered sugar. Chill 2 hours before serving.

Makes 8 servings.

Note: Use sweet flavored *Marsala all'uova* wine for this dessert.

Rum & Raisin Cheesecake

1/3 cup dark raisins
1/4 cup dark rum
4 tablespoons unsalted butter or
    margarine
8 graham crackers, crushed
3 ounces semisweet chocolate,
    chopped
2 tablespoons milk
1 cup cottage cheese
2 eggs, separated
1-2/3 (1/4-oz.) envelope unflavored
    gelatin (5 teaspoons) soaked in 3
    tablespoons water
2/3 cup whipping cream
1/4 cup sugar

To Finish:
Chocolate caraque, page 16

In a small bowl, soak raisins in rum 2 to 3 hours.

Grease an 8-inch springform cake pan. Melt butter or margarine in a small saucepan, then stir in graham cracker crumbs until well mixed.

Press mixture over bottom of greased pan. Let stand until hard.

In a small saucepan, gently heat chocolate and milk until chocolate is melted.

In a large bowl, mix cottage cheese and egg yolks until smooth. Gradually beat in chocolate mixture and rum and raisins.

In a small saucepan, gently heat gelatin until dissolved. In a small bowl, whip whipping cream until thick. Fold gelatin and whipped cream into chocolate mixture.

In a small bowl, whisk egg whites until stiff. Whisk in sugar, then fold into chocolate mixture. Spoon over crust and chill until set.

Remove cheesecake from pan and transfer to a serving plate. Decorate with chocolate caraque.

Makes 8 servings.

Chocolate-Orange Cheesecake

4 tablespoons unsalted butter
8 graham crackers
2 tablespoons light-brown sugar
1 cup cottage cheese
2 eggs, separated
Grated peel of 1 orange
8 ounces semisweet chocolate, melted,
　page 12
2 tablespoons Cointreau
2/3 cup whipping cream
1 tablespoon plus 2 teaspoons
　granulated sugar

Grease an 8-inch springform cake pan. In a small saucepan, melt butter, then stir in graham cracker crumbs and brown sugar. Press mixture over bottom of greased pan; chill until firm.

In a medium-size bowl, mix cottage cheese, egg yolks and orange peel un-til smooth. Add melted chocolate and Cointreau and mix until evenly blended.

In a small bowl, whip whipping cream until thick. Reserve 2 table-spoons for decoration; fold remaining cream into cheese mixture.

In a large bowl, whisk egg whites until stiff. Whisk in granulated sugar until thick. Add chocolate mixture and mix, using a large metal spoon; pour over prepared crust.

Spoon dots of reserved whipped cream all over cheesecake. Run a skewer through dots to create a fea-thered design. Chill 2 to 3 hours, until set.

Makes 8 servings.

Chocolate & Pistachio Marquise

1/3 cup strong coffee
2 tablespoons brandy
32 ladyfingers
6 tablespoons unsalted butter,
 softened
1/3 cup sugar
2 egg yolks
1 cup whipping cream
6 ounces semisweet chocolate, melted,
 page 12
1/4 cup pistachios, coarsely chopped

Raspberry Sauce:
8 ounces raspberries
1/3 cup powdered sugar
1 tablespoon water
1 teaspoon lemon juice

To Decorate:
Mint leaves

Line a 9" x 5" loaf pan with plastic wrap. In a shallow dish, combine coffee and brandy. Dip ladyfingers in briefly and line prepared pan, cutting to fit if necessary.

In a large bowl, beat butter and 1/2 of sugar until thick and pale. In a small bowl, whisk egg yolks with remaining sugar until thick and pale. In a third bowl, lightly whip whipping cream.

Stir cooled melted chocolate into butter mixture. Stir in egg mixture and fold in whipped cream. Carefully fold in pistachios. Pour into prepared pan and smooth top. Chill several hours or overnight.

To prepare raspberry sauce, in a blender or food processor fitted with the metal blade, process raspberries, powdered sugar and water to a puree. Press through a sieve into a bowl. Stir in lemon juice.

Turn out marquise onto a flat plate. Cut in slices and serve with raspberry sauce. Decorate with mint leaves.

Makes 8 servings.

Marbled Chiffon Pie

Almond Pastry:
1-1/2 cups all-purpose flour
2 teaspoons sugar
1/2 cup ground almonds
8 tablespoons butter, chilled
1 egg yolk
Few drops almond extract
2 teaspoons water

Chocolate Filling:
1-1/4 cups milk
3 eggs, separated
1/2 cup sugar
1-2/3 (1/4-oz.) envelope unflavored gelatin (5 teaspoons) soaked in 2 tablespoons water
2 ounces semisweet chocolate, chopped
2 ounces white chocolate, chopped

To prepare almond pastry, sift flour into a bowl. Stir in sugar and almonds. Cut in butter until mixture resembles bread crumbs. Stir in egg yolk, almond extract and water. Knead lightly, then chill 30 minutes. Preheat oven to 400F (205C).

On a lightly floured surface, roll out pastry and line a 9-inch loose-bottom flan pan. Bake blind 20 to 25 minutes, until crisp and golden; cool.

To prepare chocolate filling, in a small saucepan, heat milk until almost boiling. In a medium-size bowl, mix egg yolks and sugar. Gradually pour in hot milk, stirring constantly. Return to pan; stir over low heat until custard begins to thicken. Remove from heat and add gelatin; stir until dissolved.

Divide custard in half. Add semisweet chocolate to one half and white chocolate to other half; stir until smooth; cool.

In a small bowl, whisk egg whites until soft peaks form. Fold 1/2 of whisked egg whites into cooled semisweet chocolate mixture and remaining half into white chocolate mixture.

When chocolate mixtures are beginning to set, pour into pastry in strips. Using a fork, swirl 2 chocolate mixtures together to give a marbled effect. Chill until completely set.

Makes 8 servings.

Chocolate Praline Gâteau

Praline:
1/2 cup sugar
1/2 cup whole unblanched almonds

Meringue Rounds:
5 egg whites
1-1/4 cups sugar
1-1/3 cups ground almonds

Chocolate Butter Cream:
8 tablespoons unsalted butter,
  softened
1-1/4 cups powdered sugar, sifted
1 tablespoon water
3 ounces semisweet chocolate, melted,
  page 12

To Finish:
2 ounces semisweet chocolate, melted

Prepare praline as for Frozen Praline Ring, page 44. Grind finely in a food processor or blender.

Preheat oven to 350F (175C). Line 5 baking sheets with parchment paper and mark with an 8-inch circle.

To prepare meringue rounds, whisk egg whites until stiff, then fold in sugar and ground almonds. Spread mixture onto prepared baking sheets and bake in preheated oven 15 to 20 minutes.

Using sharp knife, trim each circle while still warm, then transfer to a wire rack to cool.

To prepare butter cream, in a medium-size bowl, beat butter and 1/2 of powdered sugar until creamy. Add remaining powdered sugar and water; beat until smooth. Stir in melted chocolate.

Mix 1/2 of praline with butter cream and sandwich meringues together. Spread side of gâteau with butter cream and cover with remaining praline. Spread remaining butter cream over top of gâteau.

To finish, in a pastry bag fitted with a writing nozzle, drizzle melted chocolate over top of gâteau.

Makes 10 to 12 servings.

Note: If you haven't enough baking sheets, use those you have in rotation. Cool meringues rounds slightly, invert onto a flat surface and peel off lining paper.

Chocolate Caramel Gâteau

4 eggs
3/4 cup sugar
1-1/4 cups all-purpose flour, sifted

Caramel:
2/3 cup water
2/3 cup sugar
1-1/2 recipes Chocolate Butter Cream,
    page 74
2 ounces semisweet chocolate, grated

Preheat oven to 375F (190C). Grease and flour 6 baking sheets and mark an 8-inch circle on each.

In a medium-size bowl, beat egg and sugar using an electric mixer until very thick and mousse-like and a trail is left when beaters are lifted, about 7 minutes.

Using a metal spoon, carefully fold in flour. Spread mixture onto prepared baking sheets and bake in preheated oven 6 to 8 minutes, until golden-brown.

Using a sharp knife, trim each round while still warm, then transfer to a wire rack to cool.

Place 1 round on an oiled baking sheet.

To prepare caramel, in a small saucepan, combine water and sugar and heat very gently until sugar is dissolved. Bring to a boil and cook rapidly until dark-brown. Pour immediately over round on baking sheet. Let stand until just on point of setting. Using an oiled knife, cut 10 to 12 sections and trim around edge.

Reserve a small amount of butter cream. Sandwich remaining rounds together with butter cream, placing caramel-covered round on top. Spread side with butter cream and coat with grated chocolate. Using a pastry bag fitted with a large fluted nozzle, pipe a rosette of reserved butter cream on each section.

Makes 10 to 12 servings

Note: If you don't have 6 baking sheets, use those you have in rotation, greasing and flouring each time.

Strawberry Gâteau

Chocolate Cake:
3 eggs
1/2 cup sugar
3/4 cup all-purpose flour, sifted
2 tablespoons unsweetened cocoa
  powder, sifted

To Finish:
8 ounces strawberries
1-1/4 cups whipping cream
1 tablespoon powdered sugar
2 tablespoons kirsch
Chocolate curls, page 16

Preheat oven to 275F (190C). Grease and line a deep 9-inch round cake pan.

To prepare cake, in a medium-size bowl, beat eggs and sugar using an electric mixer until thick and mousse-like and a trail is left when beaters are lifted. Sift flour and cocoa powder together. Using a metal spoon, carefully fold into beaten egg mixture.

Spoon into prepared pan and bake in preheated oven 25 to 30 minutes, until cake springs back when lightly pressed in center. Turn out onto a wire rack to cool.

To finish, reserve 4 strawberries. Hull and slice remaining strawberries. In a medium-size bowl, whip whipping cream with powdered sugar until thick; reserve 2/3 of whipped cream. Fold sliced strawberries into remaining whipped cream.

Cut cake in layers and sprinkle each layer with 1 tablespoon of kirsch. Place 1 layer on a serving plate and cover with strawberry cream mixture. Place other layer on top.

Cover top and side of gâteau with strawberry cream; swirl top in a decorative pattern and coat side with chocolate curls.

Using a pastry bag fitted with a fluted nozzle, pipe a decorative border of reserved whipped cream around the top of gâteau. Halve reserved strawberries and arrange on piped whipped cream.

Makes 8 servings.

Sachertorte

3 tablespoons coffee
6 ounces semisweet chocolate,
  chopped
2 tablespoons unsalted butter or
  margarine, softened
2/3 cup sugar
5 eggs, separated
1-1/4 cups all-purpose flour, sifted

Filling:
1/4 cup apricot jam
1 tablespoon water

Icing:
6 ounces semisweet chocolate,
  chopped
2 tablespoons half and half

Preheat oven to 325F (165C). Grease a deep 9-inch round cake pan and line with parchment paper.

In a small saucepan, gently heat coffee and chocolate until chocolate is melted; cool slightly.

In a large bowl, cream butter or margarine and 1/3 cup of sugar until light and fluffy. Beat in cooled chocolate and egg yolks, then stir in flour.

In a medium-size bowl, whisk egg whites until stiff, then whisk in remaining sugar. Using a metal spoon, carefully fold whisked egg whites into cake mixture. Spoon into prepared pan and bake in preheated oven 1 to 1-1/4 hours, until firm in center. Cool in pan 5 minutes, then turn out carefully onto a wire rack to cool.

Peel paper from cake. Split cake in half horizontally; sandwich together with 1/2 of apricot jam. In a small pan, heat remaining jam with water; sieve, then brush over top and side of cake.

To prepare icing, in a small saucepan, gently heat chocolate and half and half, stirring constantly, until smooth. Spread all but 2 tablespoons over top and side of cake; let stand until set.

In a pastry bag fitted with a writing nozzle, write Sacher on cake with reserved icing.

Makes 8 to 10 servings.

Yule Log

Chocolate Cake:
3 eggs
1/2 cup sugar
1/2 cup all-purpose flour
1/4 cup unsweetened cocoa powder

Vanilla Butter Icing:
4 tablespoons unsalted butter,
  softened
3/4 cup powdered sugar, sifted
2 teaspoons milk
1/2 teaspoon vanilla extract

To Finish:
1 recipe Chocolate Butter Icing,
  page 91
Sifted powdered sugar
Sprig of holly, if desired

Preheat oven to 400F (205C). Line a jellyroll pan with parchment paper and grease paper. Prepare sponge cake mixture as for Strawberry Gâteau, page 76. Spoon into prepared pan and bake in preheated oven 8 to 10 minutes, until cake springs back when lightly pressed.

Wring out a clean towel in hot water and place on a flat surface. Place waxed paper on top and sprinkle with sugar. Turn cake onto paper; peel off lining paper and trim edges.

Roll up cake from a long side, with waxed paper inside. Hold in position a few seconds, then cool on a wire rack with seam underneath.

To prepare vanilla butter icing, in a bowl, beat butter until creamy. Gradually beat in powdered sugar, then milk and vanilla; beat until smooth.

Unroll cake and remove waxed paper. Spread with all but 2 tablespoons of vanilla icing and roll up.

Cut a short diagonal slice off 1 end and attach to side of roll with chocolate butter icing.

Cover the roll with chocolate butter icing. Using a palette knife, mark icing to resemble bark of a tree.

In a pastry bag fitted with a writing nozzle, pipe concentric circles of vanilla icing on ends of log.

Sprinkle with powdered sugar to resemble snow and decorate with a holly sprig, if desired.

Makes 8 servings.

Chocolate & Chestnut Gâteau

3 ounces semisweet chocolate,
  chopped
2 tablespoons water
1 (15-1/2-oz.) can unsweetened
  chestnut puree
3 eggs, separated
1/2 cup sugar

Filling:
2/3 cup whipping cream
2 tablespoons Cointreau
1 tablespoon honey
1 to 2 tablespoons milk, if needed

To Finish:
2 tablespoons grated semisweet
  chocolate
2/3 cup whipping cream

Preheat oven to 350F (175C). Grease a jellyroll pan and line with parchment paper.

In a small saucepan, gently heat chocolate and water, stirring occasionally, until chocolate is melted. In a blender or food processor fitted with the metal blade, process melted chocolate and 1/2 of chestnut puree until smooth; set aside.

In a large bowl, whisk egg yolks and sugar until thick and creamy, then gradually whisk in chocolate mixture. In a small bowl, whisk egg whites until fairly stiff. Using a large metal spoon, carefully fold into chocolate mixture.

Spoon into pan and bake 25 to 30 minutes, until firm; cool.

To prepare filling, in a bowl, whip cream until thick. In food processor, blend remaining chestnut puree with Cointreau and honey until smooth. Fold into whipped cream, adding milk to thin, if needed.

Turn cake out of pan and cut in 3 equal strips. Using 3/4 of filling, carefully sandwich strips together. Spread remaining filling over sides of cake and coat with most of chocolate.

In a small bowl, whip whipping cream until thick. Using a pastry bag fitted with a star nozzle, pipe diagonal lines of whipped cream on top of gâteau. Sprinkle remaining grated chocolate between lines.

Makes 8 servings.

Sicilian Cassata

Cake:
1-1/2 cups self-rising flour
1 teaspoon baking powder
12 tablespoons margarine, softened
3/4 cup sugar
3 eggs

Filling:
2 cups ricotta cheese
3-1/2 ounces semisweet chocolate, grated
1/2 cup sugar
1 teaspoon vanilla extract
2 tablespoons brandy
1/2 cup chopped candied fruit
1/4 cup chopped almonds

To Decorate:
Sifted powdered sugar
Chocolate curls, page 16

Preheat oven to 375F (190C). Grease a deep 8-inch round cake pan and line with parchment paper.

To prepare cake, sift flour and baking powder into a large bowl. Add margarine, sugar and eggs and beat until smooth and creamy. Pour into prepared pan and bake in preheated oven 30 to 40 minutes, until golden-brown and firm. Turn out onto a wire rack to cool.

Wash and dry cake pan. Grease and line again.

To prepare filling, sieve ricotta cheese into a medium-size bowl. Add chocolate, sugar, vanilla and brandy; beat thoroughly until mixture is light and fluffy. Stir in candied fruit and chopped almonds.

Cut thin crust off top of cake and discard. Cut cake horizontally in 3 slices. Place 1 slice in prepared pan. Cover with 1/2 of cheese mixture. Repeat layers, finishing with cake. Press down lightly, cover with a weight and chill overnight.

To serve, turn cake out onto serving plate. Sprinkle with powdered sugar and decorate with chocolate curls.

Makes 8 servings.

Striped Chocolate Gâteau

Chocolate Ganache:
1-1/4 cups whipping cream
10 ounces semisweet chocolate,
  chopped

Chocolate Cake:
4 eggs
1/2 cup sugar
4 ounces semisweet chocolate, melted,
  page 12
1/4 cup all-purpose flour

Roulade:
2 eggs plus 1 yolk
1/3 cup sugar
1/2 cup all-purpose flour, sifted

To Decorate:
Chocolate caraque, page 16
Sifted powdered sugar

Preheat oven to 350F (175C). Grease a deep 8-inch round cake pan and a jellyroll pan and line.

To prepare ganache, heat whipping cream until almost boiling. Add chocolate and stir until melted; cool.

To prepare cake, whisk 1 egg, 3 yolks and sugar. Whisk in chocolate; sift and fold in flour. Whisk egg whites until soft peaks form. Stir 1

tablespoon into chocolate mixture, then fold in remaining egg whites. Spoon into pan. Bake 20 to 25 minutes, until just firm in center; cool. Increase heat to 425F (220C).

To prepare roulade, whisk eggs, yolk and sugar until pale and thick; fold in flour. Pour into jellyroll pan and bake in preheated oven 6 minutes or until risen and golden. Let stand 1 minute; turn out onto waxed paper dredged with powdered sugar. Roll up, enclosing paper; cool.

Whisk cooled ganache until light and fluffy. Turn out cake and cut in half. Unroll roulade, remove paper and spread with ganache. Cut in 7 (1-in.) wide strips. Roll up, joining strips to form large roll.

Spread 1 cake with ganache. Lay roulade on top. Spread thin layer of ganache on other cake; place on top of roulade. Spread remaining ganache over cake. Decorate with caraque and powdered sugar.

Makes 8 servings.

Chocolate Roulade

Roulade:
4 eggs, separated
1/2 cup sugar
4 ounces semisweet chocolate, melted, page 12, cooled

Filling:
1 cup whipping cream
5 ounces white chocolate

To Decorate:
Sifted powdered sugar
Chocolate rose leaves, page 16

Preheat oven to 350F (175C). Line a jellyroll pan with parchment paper.

To prepare roulade, in a medium-size bowl, whisk egg yolks and sugar until thick and pale. Gently fold in cooled chocolate. In small bowl, whisk egg whites until stiff. Carefully fold into chocolate mixture. Pour into prepared pan and bake in preheated oven 20 to 25 minutes, until firm. Cover with a clean towel and leave in pan overnight.

To prepare filling, in a small saucepan, heat whipping cream to just below boiling point. In a food processor fitted with the metal blade, process white chocolate until chopped. With motor running, pour hot cream through feed tube. Process 10 to 15 seconds, until mixture is smooth. Transfer to a medium-size bowl, cover with plastic wrap and chill overnight.

Whisk filling until it starts to form soft peaks.

Sprinkle waxed paper with powdered sugar. Turn out roulade onto paper. Peel away lining paper. Spread filling over roulade and roll up, starting at a short side. Place on a serving dish. Chill 2 to 3 hours.

Slice and decorate with chocolate rose leaves before serving.

Makes 6 to 8 servings.

Chocolate Truffle Cake

Cake:
1/4 cup sugar
2 eggs
1/4 cup all-purpose flour
1/4 cup unsweetened cocoa powder
1/4 cup cold strong coffee
1 tablespoon brandy

Truffle Filling:
2-1/2 cups whipping cream
15 ounces semisweet chocolate,
   melted, page 12, cooled

To Decorate:
Unsweetened cocoa powder
Powdered sugar
Chocolate shapes, page 20

Preheat oven to 425F (220C). Grease a 9-inch springform cake pan and line with parchment paper.

To prepare cake, in a medium-size bowl set over a pan of hot water, whisk sugar and eggs until pale and thick. Sift in flour and cocoa; fold gently into mixture.

Pour into prepared pan and bake in preheated oven 7 to 10 minutes or until firm to the touch. Transfer to a wire rack to cool. Wash and dry pan. Replace cake in pan when cold.

In a small bowl, mix coffee and brandy; brush over cake.

To prepare truffle filling, in a large bowl, whip whipping cream until very soft peaks form; carefully fold in cooled chocolate.

Pour chocolate mixture over cake. Chill until set.

To decorate, sift cocoa over top of cake and remove carefully from pan. Using strips of waxed paper as a guide, sift bands of powdered sugar over cake to create a striped pattern. Arrange chocolate diamonds around edge. Cut in slices with a hot knife to serve.

Makes 10 servings.

Note: It is essential that whipping cream is only whipped lightly as it thickens once chocolate is added.

Chocolate Fudge Cake

Cake:
2 tablespoons brandy
1/3 cup dark raisins
6 tablespoons unsalted butter
3 tablespoons corn syrup
6 ounces semisweet chocolate,
    chopped
16 graham crackers, crushed
1/3 cup glacé cherries, halved
1/3 cup Brazil nuts, coarsely chopped
Grated peel of 1 orange

Topping:
2 ounces semisweet chocolate, broken
    in pieces
2 tablespoons unsalted butter
Brazil nuts
Glacé cherries

In a small bowl, combine brandy and raisins. Let soak several hours or preferably overnight.

Line an 8" x 4" loaf pan with plastic wrap.

In a medium-size saucepan, gently heat butter, corn syrup and chocolate until chocolate is melted. Remove from heat. Stir in brandy and raisins, graham cracker crumbs, glacé cherries, Brazil nuts and grated orange peel.

Spoon mixture into prepared pan. Chill until firm. Turn out onto a serving plate and remove plastic wrap.

To prepare topping, in a small saucepan, melt chocolate and butter, page 12. Stir until smooth, then spread over sides and top of cake. Decorate with Brazil nuts and glacé cherries. Chill until topping has set.

Serve cut in thin slices.

Makes 10 to 12 servings.

Note: This cake is rather rich, so serve small slices.

Banana-Chocolate Fudge Cake

Cake:
12 tablespoons unsalted butter,
    softened
1-1/2 cups packed light-brown sugar
3 eggs, beaten
3 ripe bananas
2-3/4 cups all-purpose flour
1/4 cup unsweetened cocoa powder
1 tablespoon baking powder
3 tablespoons milk

Icing:
2 ounces semisweet chocolate
4 tablespoons unsalted butter
2-1/3 cups powdered sugar
1/4 cup half and half

To Decorate:
Chocolate shapes, page 20

Preheat oven to 350F (175C). Grease 2 (8-inch) round cake pans and line with parchment paper.

To prepare cake, in a large bowl, cream butter and brown sugar until light and fluffy; gradually beat in eggs. Mash bananas or process in a blender or food processor fitted with the metal blade, until completely smooth. Stir mashed bananas into brown-sugar mixture.

Sift flour, cocoa and baking powder into a medium-size bowl. Gradually stir into creamed mixture alternately with milk to yield a fairly stiff dropping consistency. Divide mixture between prepared pans and bake in preheated oven about 30 minutes, until well risen and firm to touch. Turn out onto wire racks to cool.

To prepare icing, in a medium-size saucepan, melt chocolate and butter, page 12. Remove from heat and sift in 1/2 of powdered sugar; beat until smooth. Sift in remaining powdered sugar. Stir in half and half and beat well until smooth and thick.

Sandwich cakes together with 1/4 of icing. Spread remaining icing over top and side of cake, swirling to make an attractive pattern. Decorate with chocolate triangles.

Makes 6 to 8 servings.

Rich Mocha Cake

6 ounces semisweet chocolate,
  chopped
1/4 cup cold coffee
12 tablespoons unsalted butter or
  margarine, softened
1 cup packed dark-brown sugar
4 eggs, separated
1-1/3 cups ground almonds
1/2 cup all-purpose flour, sifted

Coffee Icing:
1-1/2 cups powdered sugar
1 tablespoon coffee extract
Water

To Decorate:
8 chocolate-coated nuts, page 26

Preheat oven to 325F (165C). Grease a deep 8-inch round cake pan and line with parchment paper.

In a small saucepan, gently heat chocolate and coffee until chocolate is melted; set aside.

In a large bowl, beat butter or margarine and brown sugar until light and fluffy. Beat in egg yolks, 1 at a time, then beat in chocolate while still warm. Fold in ground almonds and flour.

In a medium-size bowl, whisk egg whites until fairly stiff. Fold 2 tablespoons into chocolate mixture to lighten it, then carefully fold in remaining whisked egg whites.

Spoon into prepared pan and bake in preheated oven 1 to 1-1/4 hours or until firm in center. Let stand in pan a few minutes, then turn out onto a wire rack to cool.

To prepare icing, sift powdered sugar into a small bowl. Add coffee extract and enough water to mix to a consistency that will coat back of spoon fairly thickly.

Spoon over cake and spread to coat top and side completely. Arrange chocolate-coated nuts around edge and let stand until set.

Makes 8 servings.

Hazelnut Cake

3 eggs, 2 separated
1/2 cup sugar
1/3 cup all-purpose flour
1 tablespoon unsweetened cocoa
  powder
1 cup hazelnuts, toasted and ground

Chocolate Icing:
1 cup whipping cream
3 ounces semisweet chocolate,
  chopped

To Finish:
1/2 cup chopped hazelnuts, toasted
1 ounce semisweet chocolate, melted,
  page 12

Preheat oven to 350F (175C). Line 2 (8-inch) cake pans with parchment paper. Grease and flour paper.

In a medium-size bowl, mix whole egg, 2 yolks and sugar, using an electric mixer, until thick and mousse-like. In a small bowl, whisk egg whites until stiff. Sift flour and cocoa together, then fold into egg mixture with ground nuts. Fold in whisked egg whites.

Spoon into prepared pans and bake in preheated oven 20 to 25 minutes, until cakes spring back when lightly pressed in center. Turn out onto a wire rack to cool.

To prepare chocolate icing, in a small saucepan, very gently heat whipping cream and chocolate, stirring constantly, until chocolate is melted. Pour into a small bowl. Cool and then chill.

Whisk icing until thick. Use 1/3 of icing to sandwich cakes together. Spread more icing around side and coat with chopped hazelnuts. Spread remaining icing over top and smooth evenly to edge.

In a pastry bag fitted with a writing nozzle, drizzle melted chocolate over top of cake.

Makes 8 to 10 servings.

Nusskuchen

12 tablespoons unsalted butter or
  margarine, softened
1 cup packed dark-brown sugar
3 eggs
1 cup self-rising flour, sifted
1 tablespoon unsweetened cocoa
  powder, sifted
3/4 cup hazelnuts, toasted and ground
2 tablespoons coffee

To Finish:
Sifted powdered sugar

Preheat oven to 350F (175C). Grease and flour a 7-1/2-inch kugelhopf pan, see note.

In a medium-size bowl, cream butter or margarine and brown sugar until light and fluffy. Beat in eggs, 1 at a time, adding 1 tablespoon of flour with second and third eggs. Fold in remaining flour, cocoa, ground hazelnuts and coffee.

Spoon into prepared pan and bake in preheated oven 45 to 50 minutes, until cake springs back when lightly pressed in center. Let stand in pan 10 minutes, then invert pan and ease cake out gently. Cool on a wire rack.

Sprinkle generously with powdered sugar to serve.

Makes 8 servings.

Note: A kugelhopf pan is a special fluted ring pan, traditionally used to cook the German yeast cake of the same name. If you do not have one, use a 9-inch ring mold instead.

Devil's Ring Cake

Cake:
6 tablespoons unsalted butter,
    softened
1 cup packed light-brown sugar
2 eggs, beaten
1/4 cup unsweetened cocoa powder
    blended with 1/3 cup boiling water,
    cooled
1 cup self-rising flour
1/2 teaspoon baking soda
Pinch of baking powder
1/3 cup dairy sour cream

Icing:
3/4 cup sugar
1/3 cup water
1 egg white
Pinch of cream of tartar

To Decorate:
Melted semisweet chocolate, page 12

Preheat oven to 350F (175C). Grease and flour a 9-inch ring pan.

To prepare cake, in a large bowl, cream butter and brown sugar until light and fluffy. Gradually beat in eggs, then stir in cooled cocoa.

Sift flour, baking soda and baking powder into a large bowl. Fold in chocolate mixture, alternating with sour cream. Pour into prepared pan and bake in preheated oven 25 to 30 minutes, until well risen and firm. Cool in pan 5 minutes, then turn out onto a wire rack to cool.

To prepare icing, in a small saucepan, combine sugar and water. Stir over low heat until sugar is dissolved. Bring to a boil and boil to soft ball stage (240F/115C) or when a small amount of syrup forms a soft ball when dropped into a cup of cold water. Remove from heat.

In a small bowl, whisk egg white until stiff; add cream of tartar. Pour hot syrup onto whisked egg white, beating constantly. Continue beating as mixture cools.

Spread icing over cake, covering it completely. Using a pastry bag fitted with a writing nozzle, pipe or drizzle lines of melted chocolate over icing.

Makes 8 to 10 servings.

Chocolate Rondelles

Cake:
1/3 cup sugar
2 eggs
1/2 cup all-purpose flour, sifted

Chocolate Icing:
1 cup whipping cream
3 ounces semisweet chocolate,
  chopped

To Finish:
1/4 cup chopped almonds, toasted
1 ounce semisweet chocolate, melted,
  page 12

Preheat oven to 375F (190C). Grease and flour 2 or 3 baking sheets.

To prepare cake, in a small bowl, beat sugar and eggs using an electric mixer until very thick and mousse-like and mixture leaves a trail when beaters are lifted. Using a metal spoon, carefully fold in flour.

Using a pastry bag fitted with a 1/2-inch plain nozzle, pipe mixture in 24 (2-1/4-inch) circles on prepared baking sheets. Bake in preheated oven 6 to 8 minutes, until golden-brown. Remove with a palette knife and cool on a wire rack.

To prepare chocolate icing, in a small saucepan, very gently heat whipping cream and chocolate, stirring constantly, until chocolate is melted. Refrigerate until cold, then whip until thick.

Sandwich 3 cakes together with some of icing, then ice top and side. Sprinkle almonds over top. Repeat with remaining cakes, icing and almonds.

In a pastry bag fitted with a writing nozzle, drizzle chocolate over top of each cake.

Makes 8 servings.

Chocolate Japonais

2 egg whites
1/2 cup hazelnuts, ground
1/2 cup sugar

Chocolate Butter Icing:
1 tablespoon unsweetened cocoa
  powder
1 tablespoon boiling water
6 tablespoons unsalted butter,
  softened
1 cup powdered sugar, sifted

Glacé Icing:
3/4 cup powdered sugar
2 teaspoons unsweetened cocoa
  powder
2 to 3 teaspoons water

To Finish:
1/4 cup hazelnuts, toasted and ground
Chocolate rose leaves, page 16

Preheat oven to 300F (150C). Line 2 baking sheets with parchment paper.

In a small bowl, whisk egg whites until stiff, then fold in ground hazelnuts and sugar. Using a pastry bag fitted with a 1/2-inch plain nozzle, pipe egg-white mixture in 16 (2-inch) circles on prepared baking sheets.

Bake in preheated oven 50 to 60 minutes; transfer to a wire rack to cool.

To prepare chocolate butter icing, blend cocoa with boiling water; cool. In a medium-size bowl, beat butter until creamy. Gradually beat in powdered sugar until smooth, then beat in cooled cocoa. Sandwich rounds together in pairs with some of icing; spread more around side. Coat side of each cake with toasted ground hazelnuts.

To make glacé icing, sift powdered sugar and cocoa into a small bowl. Add enough water to make a smooth thick icing.

Place 1 spoonful of glacé icing on each cake and spread to edge. Let stand until set. Using a pastry bag fitted with a star nozzle, pipe a rosette of remaining chocolate butter icing on each cake and decorate with a chocolate rose leaf.

Makes 8 servings.

Chocolatines

Genoise Cake:
**3 tablespoons unsalted butter or
    margarine**
3 eggs
1/3 cup sugar
3/4 cup all-purpose flour, sifted

Crème Ganache:
**8 ounces semisweet chocolate,
    chopped**
**4 tablespoons unsalted butter or
    margarine**
2/3 cup half and half

To Finish:
3/4 cup chopped almonds, browned

Preheat oven to 375F (190C). Grease an 8-inch square pan and line with parchment paper.

To prepare cake, in a small saucepan, very gently heat butter or margarine until just melted; do not allow to become hot or oily.

In a small bowl, beat eggs and sugar using an electric mixer until very thick and mousse-like. Fold in flour; when nearly incorporated, very carefully fold in butter or margarine as quickly as possible, but be careful not to deflate.

Spoon into prepared pan and bake in preheated oven 30 to 35 minutes, until cake springs back when lightly pressed. Turn out onto a wire rack to cool.

To prepare crème ganache, in a small saucepan, gently heat chocolate, butter or margarine and half and half, stirring until melted and smooth. Cool, then beat well until very smooth.

Split cake in half horizontally and sandwich with some of ganache. Using a sharp knife, cut cake in 16 squares. Spread more ganache on sides of each one and coat with chopped almonds.

In a pastry bag fitted with a fluted nozzle, pipe remaining ganache over top of each cake.

Makes 16 servings.

Chamonix

Meringue:
2 egg whites
1/2 cup sugar

Chestnut Puree:
1 pound chestnuts
3 ounces semisweet chocolate,
    chopped
1/4 cup half and half

Cream Filling:
1 egg white
1 tablespoon sugar
1 cup whipping cream, whipped

To Decorate:
Grated semisweet chocolate

Preheat oven to 250F (120C). Line 2 baking sheets with parchment paper.

To prepare meringue, in a small bowl, whisk egg whites until very stiff, then whisk in 1/2 of sugar. Carefully fold in remaining sugar.

Using a pastry bag fitted with a 1/2-inch plain nozzle, pipe meringue in 12 (3-inch) circles on prepared baking sheets. Bake in preheated oven 1-1/2 hours. Cool on baking sheets.

Meanwhile, prepare chestnut puree. Cut a slit in skin near pointed end of chestnuts. Place in a large saucepan, cover with boiling water and let stand 2 to 3 minutes. Remove from water, 1 at a time, and peel off both outer and inner skin. Return chestnuts to cleaned pan and cover with a mixture of milk and water. Cover and simmer 20 to 30 minutes or until soft. Drain and press through a sieve.

In a small pan, gently heat chocolate and half and half, stirring until chocolate is melted. Beat in chestnut puree and spoon into a pastry bag fitted with a 1/8-inch writing nozzle.

To prepare filling, in a bowl, whisk egg white until stiff, then whisk in sugar. Fold in whipping cream and set aside.

Remove meringues from baking sheets and pipe chestnut puree around top edge of each to form a nest. Fill center with cream filling and sprinkle with grated chocolate.

Makes 12 servings.

Ginger & Chocolate Meringues

4 egg whites
1-1/4 cups sugar
4 ounces semisweet chocolate, grated

Filling:
1-1/4 cups whipping cream
1 tablespoon syrup from stem ginger
3 pieces stem ginger, finely chopped
1/2 teaspoon ground cinnamon

To Decorate:
Chocolate leaves, page 16

Preheat oven to 250F (120C). Line 2 baking sheets with parchment paper.

In a medium-size bowl, whisk egg whites until stiff. Whisk in 1/2 of sugar. Fold in remaining sugar with grated chocolate.

Pipe or spoon 16 tablespoons of meringue mixture onto prepared baking sheets, allowing room to spread slightly. Bake in preheated oven 1-1/2 hours or until dry. Transfer to wire racks to cool.

To prepare filling, in a small bowl, whip whipping cream until thick. Stir in ginger syrup, then add chopped ginger and cinnamon.

Use filling to sandwich meringues together. Decorate with chocolate leaves to serve.

Makes 8 servings.

Variations: Omit grated chocolate from meringue mixture. When meringues are cooked, melt 4 ounces semisweet chocolate, page 12. Dip bottom of each cooled meringue shell into melted chocolate. Let set on waxed paper. Sandwich together with ginger cream.

Or pipe meringues in fingers using a pastry bag fitted with a 3/4-inch plain or fluted nozzle. Dip ends of meringues into melted chocolate when cool. Let set on waxed paper. Sandwich together with ginger cream.

Chocolate Cream Drops

Drops:
3 eggs
1/2 cup sugar
3/4 cup plus 2 tablespoons
   all-purpose flour
2 tablespoons unsweetened cocoa
   powder

Chocolate Ganache:
1 cup whipping cream
8 ounces semisweet chocolate,
   chopped

To Decorate:
2 ounces white chocolate, melted,
   page 12

Preheat oven to 375F (190C). Grease 4 baking sheets and line with parchment paper.

To prepare drops, in a medium-size bowl, whisk eggs and sugar until the mixture is thick and light and whisk leaves a trail when lifted. Sift flour and cocoa onto mixture; fold in gently.

Drop teaspoonfuls of mixture onto prepared baking sheets, leaving a 2-inch space between them. Bake in preheated oven in 2 batches 10 minutes or until firm. Let stand on baking sheets a few minutes, then transfer to wire racks to cool.

To prepare chocolate ganache, in a medium-size saucepan, heat whipping cream until almost boiling. Remove from heat and add chocolate; stir until smooth. Cool, then whisk until thick and light. Sandwich drops together with chocolate ganache.

To decorate, using a pastry bag fitted with a writing nozzle, drizzle white chocolate over top of each drop.

Makes 20 pieces.

Note: Chocolate cream drops are at their best about 2 hours after filling.

Variations: Drizzle with semisweet chocolate rather than white chocolate, or dust drops with sifted powdered sugar.

Barcettos

Almond Pastry:
1/2 cup all-purpose flour
1/4 cup ground almonds
2 tablespoons unsalted butter,
   softened
2 tablespoons sugar
1 egg yolk
1 teaspoon water

Frangipane:
1/4 cup sugar
1/3 cup ground almonds
1 egg white
Few drops of almond extract

To Finish:
1 ounce semisweet chocolate, melted,
   page 12

Preheat oven to 375F (190C).

To prepare pastry, sift flour onto a cool work surface and sprinkle with ground almonds. Make a well in center and put in butter, sugar, egg yolk and water.

Using fingertips of 1 hand, work these ingredients together, then draw in flour and almonds.

Knead lightly until smooth; wrap in plastic wrap and chill 1 hour.

On a lightly floured surface, roll out pastry thinly and line 12 (3-inch) barquette molds. Prick bottoms and chill 15 minutes.

To prepare frangipane, combine all ingredients in a small bowl and mix thoroughly. Divide mixture among molds, place on a baking sheet and bake in preheated oven 12 to 15 minutes. Transfer to a wire rack to cool.

In a pastry bag fitted with a writing nozzle, drizzle chocolate on top of each barquette.

Makes 12 servings.

Note: Almond pastry should be rolled very thinly.

Chocolate Almond Tartlets

Pâte Sucrée:
1/2 cup all-purpose flour
2 tablespoons unsalted butter, softened
2 tablespoons sugar
1 egg yolk

Filling:
1/3 cup packed dark-brown sugar
2 tablespoons corn syrup
4 tablespoons unsalted butter
1 tablespoon water
1 cup slivered almonds, chopped and toasted
2 ounces semisweet chocolate, melted, page 12

Preheat oven to 375F (190C).

To prepare pâte sucrée, sift flour onto a cool work surface. Make a well in center and put in butter, sugar and egg yolk. Using fingertips of 1 hand, work these ingredients together, then draw in flour. Knead lightly until smooth, then chill 1 hour.

On a lightly floured surface, roll out pastry very thinly and line 12 tart-let molds. Prick bottoms and chill 15 minutes. Press a square of foil into each tartlet and bake blind 8 to 10 minutes, until golden. Remove foil and cool on a wire rack.

To prepare filling, combine brown sugar, corn syrup, butter and water in a small heavy-bottom saucepan. Heat gently, stirring constantly, until sugar is dissolved. Boil 5 to 7 minutes to 240F (115C) or until a small amount of mixture forms a soft ball when dropped into cold water. Stir in all but 1 tablespoon of almonds. Spoon filling into pastry cups before it begins to set.

Chop reserved almonds finely. Spread melted chocolate over filling and sprinkle chopped nuts around edge of each tartlet.

Makes 10 servings.

Note: Pâte sucrée should be rolled very thinly.

Strawberry-Chocolate Tarts

Pastry:
7 tablespoons butter, softened
2 teaspoons powdered sugar
1 egg yolk
1 tablespoon water
1-1/2 cups all-purpose flour

Chocolate Filling:
4 tablespoons unsalted butter,
  softened
1/4 cup sugar
1 egg, beaten
2 ounces semisweet chocolate, grated
1/2 cup ground almonds

Topping:
1 tablespoon plus 1 teaspoon red
  currant jelly
1 teaspoon kirsch
8 ounces strawberries, hulled, halved

To prepare pastry, in a medium-size bowl, cream butter and powdered sugar until soft and light. In a small bowl, mix egg yolk and water; gradually stir into creamed mixture. Sift flour into mixture and mix to a smooth dough with a round-bladed knife. Wrap in plastic wrap and chill 1 hour.

Preheat oven to 375F (190C).

On a lightly floured surface, roll out pastry thinly and line 4 (4-inch) quiche pans.

To prepare filling, in a small bowl, beat butter and sugar until creamy, then beat in egg. Stir in chocolate; add ground almonds and mix to a soft dropping consistency. Divide among pastry shells. Bake in preheated oven 20 to 25 minutes, until filling is set and pastry is crisp.

To prepare topping, in a small saucepan, gently heat red currant jelly, stirring until completely dissolved. Stir in kirsch. Brush over chocolate tarts while still warm. Arrange strawberry halves on top and brush with remaining red currant jelly. Transfer to a wire rack to cool.

Makes 4 servings.

Chocolate Pastry Tartlets

Pastry:
3/4 cup plus 2 tablespoons
  all-purpose flour
2 tablespoons unsweetened cocoa
  powder
4 tablespoons butter, softened
2 tablespoons powdered sugar, sifted
1 egg yolk
Pinch of salt

Filling:
1/3 cup whipping cream
1 cup strawberry fromage frais, see
  note
1 teaspoon triple-strength rose water
6 ounces red currants

To Decorate:
Frosted leaves, if desired

Preheat oven to 350F (175C).

To prepare pastry, sift flour and cocoa into a large bowl. Add butter, powdered sugar, egg yolk and salt. Work ingredients together with fingers until mixture forms a firm dough. Wrap in plastic wrap and chill 30 minutes until firm.

On a lightly floured surface, roll out pastry thinly and line 12 tartlet pans; prick bottoms. Press a piece of foil into each tartlet. Bake in preheated oven 10 minutes. Remove foil and bake 10 minutes more or until pastry is golden and firm to touch. Transfer to a wire rack to cool.

To prepare filling, in a medium-size bowl, whip whipping cream lightly. Fold in fromage frais and rose water. Place 1 spoonful of filling in each tartlet and arrange red currants on top. Decorate with frosted leaves, if desired. Serve as soon as possible.

Makes 12 servings.

Note: If strawberry flavored fromage frais is unobtainable, use crème fraîche or plain fromage frais.

Pains au Chocolat

2 cups bread flour
1 teaspoon salt
2/3 (1/4-oz.) package fast-rising yeast
  (2 teaspoons)
3/4 cup milk
1 tablespoon plus 2 teaspoons sugar
1 tablespoon vegetable oil
7 tablespoons butter
1/2 cup semisweet chocolate pieces (3
  oz.)

Glaze:
1 egg yolk
1 tablespoon plus 1 teaspoon milk

Sift flour and salt into a large bowl. Stir in yeast. Make well in center.

In a small saucepan, heat milk to 120F (50C) to 130F (55C). Add sugar and oil; stir until sugar is dissolved. Add to flour; mix well. Knead lightly on floured surface until smooth.

Place dough in cleaned bowl, cover and let rise in a warm place 1 to 2 hours, until tripled in size.

Knead again, return to bowl, cover and let rise again 1 to 2 hours or until doubled in size.

Knead, then roll in a rectangle 3 times as long as it is wide.

Divide butter in thirds. Dot 1 portion in small pieces over top 2/3 of dough, leaving a 1/2-inch border. Fold lower third up and top third down; press edges with rolling pin to seal. Give dough a half turn and roll in a rectangle as before. Repeat process twice with remaining butter. Fold dough in half, place in an oiled bowl, cover and chill 1 hour.

Cut dough in half; roll out each half to a 12" x 6" rectangle. Cut in 4 (3" x 6") rectangles.

Sprinkle a line of chocolate pieces along short end of each rectangle. Roll up jellyroll style. Place rolls seam side-down on a buttered baking sheet and let stand in a warm place until double in size. Preheat oven to 425F (220C).

In a small bowl, mix egg yolk and milk; brush over rolls. Bake in center of oven 15 to 20 minutes, until well risen.

Makes 8 servings.

Walnut & Chocolate Fingers

5 sheets filo pastry
4 tablespoons unsalted butter, melted

Filling:
1-1/4 cups walnut pieces, coarsely
  ground
2 tablespoons sugar
1/2 teaspoon ground cinnamon
2 ounces semisweet chocolate, grated

To Decorate:
1 tablespoon powdered sugar

Preheat oven to 325F (165C). Grease 2 baking sheets.

To prepare filling, in a small bowl, mix ground walnuts, sugar, cinnamon and grated chocolate.

Cut each sheet of filo pastry in 4 (9" x 7") rectangles. Pile on top of each other and cover with a towel to prevent drying out.

Brush a filo rectangle with melted butter. Spread 1 teaspoon of filling along one short end. Fold long sides in, slightly over filling. Roll up from filling end. Place on prepared baking sheet with seam underneath; brush with melted butter. Repeat with remaining pastry and filling. Bake in preheated oven 20 minutes or until very lightly colored.

Transfer to a wire rack to cool. Dust with sifted powdered sugar to serve.

Makes 24 pieces.

Variations:
Almond Fingers: Substitute ground almonds for walnuts and orange flower water for cinnamon.

Pistachio Fingers: Substitute finely chopped pistachios for walnuts and rose water for cinnamon.

Pine Nut Fingers: Substitute finely chopped pine nuts for walnut and orange flower water for cinnamon.

Pineapple-Ginger Florentines

6 tablespoons unsalted butter or
  margarine
1/4 cup corn syrup
1/4 cup all-purpose flour, sifted
1 ounce angelica, coarsely chopped
1/4 cup crystallized ginger, coarsely
  chopped
1/2 cup sliced almonds, coarsely
  chopped
1/3 cup glacé pineapple, coarsely
  chopped
1 teaspoon lemon juice
4 ounces semisweet chocolate, melted,
  page 12

Preheat oven to 350F (175C). Line 2 baking sheets with parchment paper.

In a medium-size saucepan, heat butter or margarine and corn syrup until melted, then stir in flour, angelica, ginger, almonds, glacé pineapple and lemon juice.

Drop walnut-size mounds of mixture well apart on prepared baking sheets and flatten with a fork. Bake in preheated oven 8 to 10 minutes. Cool 1 minute, then transfer to a wire rack to cool completely.

Spread chocolate over bottom of each florentine. Place cookies, chocolate side-up, on a wire rack and mark chocolate in lines with a small palette knife. Let stand until set.

Makes about 14 pieces.

Variation: Replace ginger with dried apricots and use milk chocolate instead of semisweet chocolate.

Almond Fingers

1 egg white
1-1/4 cups ground almonds
2 tablespoons ground rice
2/3 cup sugar
Rice paper
1 ounce semisweet chocolate, melted,
   page 12

Preheat oven to 325F (165C).

In a medium-size bowl, lightly whisk egg white, then add ground almonds, ground rice and sugar. Mix to a firm consistency, then divide in 4 pieces. Roll each piece in a sausage shape about 16 inches long. Arrange close together so that long sides are touching, forming a four-fold long strip.

Cut strip diagonally in 1-1/4-inch widths. Lift each piece onto rice paper, spacing a little apart to allow for spreading and place on a baking sheet.

Bake in preheated oven 20 minutes, until golden-brown, then transfer to a wire rack to cool. Tear off any excess rice paper.

In a pastry bag fitted with a writing nozzle, drizzle chocolate over fingers.

Makes about 15 pieces.

Hazelnut-Chocolate Crescents

16 tablespoons unsalted butter,
  softened
1/3 cup sugar
1 egg yolk
1 teaspoon rum
2 cups blanched hazelnuts, ground
About 2 cups all-purpose flour
1/2 cup cornstarch
2 tablespoons unsweetened cocoa
  powder

To Decorate:
1/3 cup powdered sugar, sifted

Preheat oven to 350F (175C). Grease several baking sheets.

In a large bowl, cream butter and sugar until pale and fluffy. Beat in egg yolk and rum. Stir in ground hazelnuts. Sift 2 cups flour, cornstarch and cocoa together over mixture. Stir in dry ingredients, adding a little more flour, if necessary, to make a firm dough.

With lightly floured hands, break off walnut-size pieces of dough. Roll each in a 3-inch length, tapering in pointed ends. Shape in crescents and place on prepared baking sheets. Bake in preheated oven 20 to 25 minutes, until firm. Transfer to wire racks to cool.

Gently toss crescents in powdered sugar to coat completely.

Makes 40 pieces.

Note: Grind hazelnuts in a food processor fitted with the metal blade or blender if possible. Do not use ready ground hazelnuts as they are too fine.

Variation: Freshly ground almonds or walnuts may be used instead of hazelnuts.

Almond & Chocolate Tuiles

4 tablespoons unsalted butter
2 egg whites
1/2 cup sugar
1/3 cup all-purpose flour
2 tablespoons unsweetened cocoa
powder
1/4 cup sliced almonds
Grated peel of 1 orange

Preheat oven to 350F (175C). Grease 2 or 3 baking sheets and a rolling pin.

In a small saucepan, melt butter and cool. In a small bowl, using a fork, whisk egg whites and sugar until mixture is frothy. Sift flour and cocoa into egg whites. Add sliced almonds and orange peel; mix with a fork. Add cooled butter and mix thoroughly.

Drop teaspoonfuls of mixture onto prepared baking sheets, leaving 5 inches of space between each. Using a palette knife, spread each one out slightly.

Bake in preheated oven, 1 sheet at a time, 8 to 10 minutes, until edges feel firm.

Lift cookies off carefully with a palette knife and place on a rolling pin while still warm. Let set 2 minutes until set in a curved shape; transfer to a wire rack to cool completely. Store in an airtight container.

Makes 18 pieces.

Variations: To make tulip shaped baskets for serving ice cream, shape cooked tuiles over small greased bowls or glasses.

Pecan & Chocolate Chip Cookies

8 tablespoons unsalted butter,
   softened
1/4 cup granulated sugar
1/3 cup packed light-brown sugar
1 egg
1 teaspoon vanilla extract
1 cup all-purpose flour
2 tablespoons unsweetened cocoa
   powder
1/2 teaspoon baking soda
1/2 cup chocolate pieces (4 oz.)
1/2 cup pecans, coarsely chopped

Preheat oven to 350F (175C). Grease 2 or 3 baking sheets.

In a large bowl, cream butter and sugars until light and fluffy. In another bowl, beat egg and vanilla; gradually beat into creamed mixture.

Sift flour, cocoa and baking soda over creamed mixture; stir in carefully. Stir in chocolate pieces and pecans.

Drop teaspoonfuls of mixture, well apart, on prepared baking sheets.

Bake in preheated oven 10 to 15 minutes or until mixture has spread and cookies are beginning to feel firm. Carefully transfer to wire racks to cool and become crisp. Store in an airtight container.

Makes about 28 cookies.

Variations:
Vanilla Chocolate Chip Cookies: Omit cocoa and add an extra 2 tablespoons flour.

Mocha Chocolate Chip Cookies: Add 2 teaspoons instant coffee granules with flour and cocoa.

Fruit & Chocolate Chip Cookies: Replace nuts with 1/3 cup each chopped dried apricots and pineapple and coconut flakes.

Chocolate Muffins

2-1/4 cups all-purpose flour
1 tablespoon baking powder
1/2 teaspoon salt
1 tablespoon plus 2 teaspoons sugar
1/4 cup semisweet chocolate pieces
  (2 oz.)
4 tablespoons butter, melted, cooled
1 egg, beaten
1 cup milk

Orange Butter:
8 tablespoons unsalted butter,
  softened
2 tablespoons powdered sugar
2 tablespoons fresh orange juice
Grated peel of 1/2 orange

Preheat oven to 400F (205C). Thoroughly grease a deep 12-cup muffin pan or line with paper baking cups.

Sift flour, baking powder and salt into a large bowl. Stir in sugar and chocolate pieces.

In a small bowl, mix cooled butter, egg and milk. Pour into dry ingredients and stir until flour is just moistened but looks lumpy. Spoon mixture into prepared cups. Bake in preheated oven 15 to 20 minutes, until well risen and golden-brown. Cool in cups 5 minutes before serving.

To prepare orange butter, in a small bowl, beat all ingredients until light and fluffy.

Serve muffins warm with orange butter.

Makes 12 muffins.

Note: If serving muffins for breakfast, mix dry ingredients in a bowl and make orange butter the day before. It takes only a matter of minutes to stir in liquid and bake muffins the next morning.

Lebkuchen

Rice paper
3 eggs
1 cup sugar
1 cup all-purpose flour
1 teaspoon ground cinnamon
1/4 teaspoon ground cloves
1/4 teaspoon grated nutmeg
1/2 teaspoon ground cardamom
1-3/4 cups unblanched almonds,
  coarsely ground
2 tablespoons candied lemon peel,
  finely chopped
2 tablespoons candied orange peel,
  finely chopped
1-1/2 ounces semisweet chocolate,
  grated
1/2 teaspoon grated lemon peel
1/2 teaspoon grated orange peel
2 teaspoons triple-strength rose water

Icing:
1 egg white
2 teaspoons unsweetened cocoa
  powder blended with 1 tablespoon
  boiling water
3/4 cup powdered sugar
2 tablespoons sugar crystals

Preheat oven to 325F (165C). Line bottom of a jellyroll pan with rice paper.

In a large bowl, whisk eggs and sugar until mixture is thick and light and whisk leaves a trail when lifted. Sift in flour and spices. Stir in almonds, candied citrus peels, grated chocolate and grated lemon and orange peels.

Spread mixture evenly in prepared pan and brush with rose water. Bake in preheated oven 30 to 35 minutes, until firm.

To prepare icing, in a small bowl, stir egg white into cooled cocoa. Sift in powdered sugar and mix thoroughly. Spread icing over cake while still warm. Sprinkle with sugar crystals. Return to oven about 5 minutes. Cut in squares when cold.

Makes 24 pieces.

Panforte di Siena

1/3 cup glacé cherries, quartered
1/3 cup candied orange peel, finely
    chopped
1/3 cup candied lemon peel, finely
    chopped
2 tablespoons crystallized ginger,
    coarsely chopped
3/4 cup sliced almonds
3/4 cup hazelnuts, toasted and
    coarsely ground
1/2 cup all-purpose flour
1/4 cup unsweetened cocoa powder
1 teaspoon ground cinnamon
1/4 teaspoon ground cloves
1/3 cup honey
1/2 cup granulated sugar
1 teaspoon orange flower water

To Decorate:
Powdered sugar

Preheat oven to 325F (165C). Thoroughly grease bottom of an 8-inch loose-bottom cake or flan pan. Line bottom with waxed paper; grease again.

In a medium-size bowl, mix glacé cherries, orange and lemon peel, ginger, almonds and hazelnuts. Sift in flour, cocoa, cinnamon and cloves and mix thoroughly; set aside.

In a medium-size saucepan, heat honey, granulated sugar and orange flower water until sugar is dissolved. Bring to a boil and boil steadily until mixture reaches soft ball stage (240F/ 115C). To test, drop a small amount of syrup into a cup of cold water; it should form a soft ball.

Quickly remove pan from heat, stir in prepared dry ingredients and mix thoroughly. Spoon into prepared pan, spread evenly and bake in preheated oven 30 minutes.

Cool in pan. Turn out and peel away waxed paper. Sift powdered sugar over top and cut wedges to serve.

Makes 12 to 16 servings.

Cream Truffles

1/3 cup whipping cream
1 vanilla bean
1 tablespoon plus 2 teaspoons sugar
1 egg yolk
5 ounces semisweet chocolate,
    chopped
2 tablespoons unsalted butter
2 teaspoons crème de cacao

Coating:
1 tablespoon plus 1 teaspoon
    unsweetened cocoa powder
2 teaspoons powdered sugar

Line a jellyroll pan with parchment paper.

In a medium-size saucepan, bring whipping cream and vanilla bean almost to a boil. Remove from heat, cover and set aside 30 minutes. Remove vanilla bean.

In a small bowl, whisk sugar and egg yolk until pale and thick; whisk into whipping cream in pan. Return pan to heat and gently heat without boiling. Add chocolate and butter, stirring until mixture is smooth. Stir in crème de cacao. Pour into prepared pan and chill 1 hour or until firm.

To prepare coating, sift cocoa and powdered sugar onto a plate. Pull off small pieces of chilled truffle mixture and roll in balls. Roll each ball in sifted cocoa mixture and place in paper cups, if desired. Refrigerate and eat within 2 to 3 days.

Makes 20 pieces.

Variations: Use brandy, rum or other liqueur, such as Tia Maria, instead of crème de cacao.

Truffles may be coated in melted semisweet or white chocolate, or rolled in crushed praline or nuts, as an alternative to cocoa and powdered sugar. Drizzled contrasting chocolate makes an attractive finish for chocolate-coated truffles.

Collettes

9 ounces semisweet chocolate
1/2 teaspoon sunflower oil
2/3 cup whipping cream
Finely grated peel of 1/2 orange
1 tablespoon Cointreau

To Decorate:
Blanched almonds
Chopped nuts
Chocolate-coated nuts, page 26

In a small saucepan, melt 5 ounces of chocolate with oil, page 12.

Using double petit four paper cups, brush chocolate evenly over inside of 20 cups. Chill until set. Apply a second coat of chocolate, remelting if necessary. Chill until completely set.

In a small saucepan, heat whipping cream with grated orange peel until boiling. Remove from heat, add remaining chocolate and stir until smooth. Return pan to heat and stir until mixture begins to bubble. Grad-ually stir in Cointreau; cool.

Peel paper cups off chocolate cups.

Beat cooled chocolate cream until thick. In a pastry bag fitted with a fluted nozzle, pipe chocolate cream into chocolate cups. Decorate with whole, chopped and chocolate-coated nuts. Refrigerate and use within 2 or 3 days.

Makes 20 pieces.

Variations: Use a small amount of coffee extract, praline powder or finely chopped nuts in place of grated orange peel.

Use an alternative liqueur, rum or brandy instead of Cointreau.

Prepare chocolate cups with chocolate or use white chocolate in filling instead of semisweet chocolate.

Chocolate Nut Fudge

8 tablespoons unsalted butter
1/4 cup coffee
2 tablespoons unsweetened cocoa
  powder
2 tablespoons corn syrup
3 cups sugar
3/4 cup plus 2 tablespoons sweetened
  condensed milk
1 cup chopped pecans

Grease an 11" x 7" baking pan.

In a large saucepan, combine butter, coffee, cocoa, corn syrup and sugar. Heat gently, stirring occasionally, until sugar is dissolved; do not allow to boil at this stage or finished fudge will crystallize and will not have a smooth texture.

Add condensed milk and bring to a boil, stirring constantly. Boil steadily 5 to 10 minutes, until bubbles look like erupting volcanos. Cook to soft ball stage (240F/115C) or when a small amount of mixture forms a soft ball when dropped into a cup of cold water.

Cool until bubbling stops. Beat well about 5 minutes, until mixture begins to thicken. This will give a smooth texture.

Add chopped pecans and mix well. Pour into prepared baking pan and let stand 30 minutes, until half set. Mark in 1-inch squares with a sharp knife and let stand until cold.

Cut in squares, remove from baking pan and store in candy jars or decorative boxes.

Makes 1-1/2 pounds.

Torrone Molle

12 tablespoons unsalted butter,
   softened
6 ounces semisweet chocolate, melted,
   page 12
2/3 cup walnut halves, coarsely
   ground
1/3 cup blanched almonds, coarsely
   ground
1/3 cup hazelnuts, coarsely ground
1/2 cup sugar
3 tablespoons water
1 egg beaten with 1 yolk
1 tablespoon brandy
6 ounces Petit Beurre cookies

To Decorate:
Chocolate-coated blanched almonds,
   page 26

Oil a jelly-roll pan.

In a large bowl, beat butter and melted chocolate until smooth. Stir in all ground nuts.

In a small saucepan, heat sugar and water until sugar is dissolved. Boil steadily until mixture reaches soft ball stage (240F/115C) or until a small amount of mixture forms a soft ball when dropped into cold water. Cool a few minutes, then beat vigorously and pour into chocolate mixture, stirring until smooth. Stir in beaten egg and brandy.

Break cookies in small almond-size pieces. Stir gently into mixture. Turn into prepared pan and press to flatten. Cover and chill overnight. Remove from refrigerator just before serving and cut in diamond shapes. Decorate diamonds with chocolate-coated almonds.

Makes 24 pieces.

Note: Instead of cutting in squares, torrone mixture may be spooned into a glass serving bowl and served as a firm, rich chocolate pudding.

Variation: Substitute 1-2/3 cups ground almonds for mixture of nuts to give a slightly different texture to torrone.

Praline & Sesame Sweets

1/2 cup sugar
3/4 cup whole unblanched almonds
1 tablespoon sesame seeds, toasted
2 ounces semisweet chocolate, melted,
  page 12

Oil a baking sheet.

In a small heavy-bottom saucepan, heat sugar and almonds very gently until sugar is dissolved. Cook gently until almonds begin to pop and turn brown and caramel is a rich brown color; shake pan so that almonds are coated with caramel.

Pour in sesame seeds and shake pan to mix. Pour onto oiled baking sheet and let stand until hard.

Break praline in large pieces and half dip in warm melted chocolate.

Shake off excess; place on waxed paper to set.

Any broken pieces of praline can be coarsely chopped, mixed into remaining chocolate and spooned in mounds on waxed paper.

Makes 20 to 24 pieces.

Note: When exposed to a damp atmosphere, the praline may become rather sticky. To prevent this happening, coat completely with chocolate.

Variation: Replace almonds with hazelnuts and dip into chocolate to coat completely, if desired.

Chocolate Fruit & Nuts

4 ounces semisweet chocolate,
  chopped
6 dates, pitted
8 dried apricots
1/2 cup slivered almonds

In a small heatproof bowl set over a pan of hot water, very gently heat chocolate until melted.

Using a skewer, dip each fruit into melted chocolate. Lift out and allow any excess chocolate to drop off. Place on waxed paper, carefully easing fruit off skewer with a second skewer. Let stand until chocolate has set.

Toast almonds. Add to remaining chocolate and mix until well coated. Spoon onto waxed paper in 6 small circles and let stand until chocolate has set.

Makes 20 pieces.

Note: If desired, dates may be stuffed with almond paste before dipping.

Variations:
Chocolate Marzipan Balls: Shape 4 ounces almond paste in cherry-size balls, and dip into melted chocolate to coat.

Chocolate Cherries: Divide 2 ounces almond paste in 10 pieces and mold each piece around a glacé cherry to cover completely. Dip into melted chocolate to coat.

Chocolate Syrup

1-1/4 cup sugar
1-1/4 cups water
3/4 cup unsweetened cocoa powder

To Serve:
Milk
Vanilla ice cream
Whipped cream
Sifted unsweetened cocoa powder

In a small saucepan, heat sugar and water until sugar is dissolved. Bring to a boil; boil 3 minutes, stirring occasionally. Whisk in cocoa and continue whisking over moderate heat until smooth. Cool and refrigerate syrup until needed.

For each serving, whisk 1 cup milk and 3 tablespoons chilled chocolate syrup.

Pour into a chilled glass, add a scoop of ice cream and top with a generous spoonful of whipped cream. Sprinkle with cocoa and serve immediately.

Makes 2 cups syrup.

Note: This syrup can be refrigerated several weeks and used as needed. It is an excellent topping for ice cream.

Hot Chocolate

1-1/2 ounces semisweet chocolate, chopped
1-1/4 cups milk

Place chocolate in a medium-size bowl. In a small saucepan, bring milk to a boil. Pour about 1/4 of milk into chocolate. Let stand until chocolate has softened, then whisk until smooth. Return remaining milk to heat and bring back to a boil. Pour onto chocolate, whisking constantly. Serve immediately.

Makes 1 to 2 servings.

Variations:
Rum Toddy: Melt chocolate as above. Whisk in 2 tablespoons dark rum. Continue as above. To serve, top with whipped cream and a little grated nutmeg.

Spiced Chocolate: Add a good pinch each of grated nutmeg, ground allspice and ground cinnamon to milk while heating in saucepan. To serve, top with whipped cream and grated chocolate.

Hot Jucalette: Add 1 tablespoon sugar and 1/4 teaspoon ground cinnamon to milk while heating in saucepan. To serve, pour 1 tablespoon whiskey into each heatproof glass; pour over spiced milk. Top with whipped cream and fine shreds of cinnamon stick.

Mocha: Dissolve 1 tablespoon instant coffee granules in milk while heating in saucepan. To serve, pour 1 tablespoon whipping cream over top of each serving and sprinkle with chopped walnuts.

Chocolate Cocktails

CRÈME DE MENTHE FRAPPÉ
1/2 jigger crème de menthe
1 jigger crème de cacao
1 jigger whipping cream
Crushed ice
Sprig of mint to decorate

Place crème de menthe, crème de cacao and cream in a cocktail shaker and shake thoroughly.

Half fill a stemmed glass with crushed ice and pour cocktail over ice. Decorate with mint.

Makes 1 serving.

Variation: Use Cointreau instead of crème de menthe.

RUM VELVET
1 jigger dark crème de cacao
1 jigger dark rum
1 jigger whipping cream

To Finish:
Grated semisweet chocolate

Pour crème de cacao and rum into a cocktail glass and stir to mix. Slowly and carefully pour whipping cream over back of a teaspoon into glass, so that it floats on top.

Sprinkle with grated chocolate to serve.

Makes 1 serving.

BRANDY ALEXANDER
1 jigger crème de cacao
1 jigger brandy
1 jigger whipping cream
Crushed ice
Grated nutmeg

Place crème de cacao, brandy and whipping cream in a cocktail shaker. Add crushed ice and shake well.

Strain into a cocktail glass and sprinkle with grated nutmeg to serve.

Makes 1 serving.

Chocolate Toddies

MEXICANAS
1 ounce semisweet chocolate, grated
1-1/4 cups hot coffee
2 teaspoons dark-brown sugar
1 tablespoon dark rum
2 tablespoons whipping cream,
    whipped
Chocolate curls, page 16, to decorate

Place chocolate, coffee and sugar in a blender or food processor and process until blended. Add rum and pour into 2 heatproof mugs. Top with whipped cream and sprinkle with chocolate curls. Serve immediately.

Makes 2 servings.

COFFEE CALYPSO
2 tablespoons dark crème de cacao
1 teaspoon dark-brown sugar
1/2 cup hot coffee
2 tablespoons whipping cream

To Finish:
Instant coffee granules

Pour crème de cacao into a heatproof mug, then add sugar and coffee. Stir well, then slowly and carefully pour whipping cream over back of a teaspoon into glass so that it floats.
    Sprinkle with coffee granules and serve immediately.

Makes 1 serving.

HOT CHOCOLATE NOG
3 ounces semisweet chocolate,
    chopped
1-3/4 cups hot milk
1 tablespoon sugar
1 egg
3 tablespoons brandy

Place chocolate, hot milk and sugar in a blender or food processor and process until chocolate is melted. Add egg and brandy and process 20 seconds.
    Pour into 2 heatproof mugs and serve immediately.

Makes 2 servings.

INDEX

PRINTED IN BELGIUM BY
proost
INTERNATIONAL BOOK PRODUCTION